Bert Hellinger

Looking Into The Souls

of Children

The Hellinger Pedagogy in Action

Hellinger® publications

Published by
Hellinger® *publications*
Sonnleitstr. 37
83404 Bischofswiesen
Germany
Postfach 2120 •
83462 Berchtesgaden
www.hellinger.com

Translated by Angelika Schenk
Edited and Revised by Suzi Tucker
Original Cover by Manuela Schroll
Original Typesetting and Layout by Beyer Werbung+Druck
Cover Design, Layout, and Text Review by Cole Tucker-Walton

ISBN 978-3-942808-30-9

11 10 9 8 7 6 5 4 3 2 **1**
2017 2016 2015 **2014**

Foreword

I am excited to write a foreword for *Looking Into the Souls of Children* as an excuse to accomplish two things: to provide a bit of a roadmap for the unusual landscape you are about to enter and to pay homage to my most esteemed teacher, inspiration and friend.

I have known Bert Hellinger since 1998, having worked on his first original contribution published in English, *Love's Hidden Symmetry*. Coauthored by Hunter Beaumont and Gunthard Weber, the book provided an initial glimpse of what Bert Hellinger was beginning to explore. I often tell of how after being involved in the project for a year, I was pretty sure I understood everything there was to understand about the perspective and the purpose – until I attended a workshop.

It was at the Family Therapy (now Psychotherapy) Networker Conference in Washinton, DC, that I met Bert in person. I attended his workshop. I had dinner with him. I quickly realized that what I had understood until that moment was but a sliver of what he was thinking, doing, providing a portal for.

So, now it's been 15 or 16 years since that first meeting. I have worked on too many of Bert's books to count. The gratitude I have for this ongoing opportunity is beyond my capacity for language.

And because the horizon grows wider with each step we take toward it, there is always so much more to tell -- to know, to touch upon, to savor, to let join with all other knowledge. Each of Bert's books is a place in which he reflects and expresses not solely what comes from his mind but what comes through his being.

Reading Bert's writing has taught me to read in a different way. Over the years I find that I pay evermore attention to the energy of language, to the attunement of character and circumstances, and to the long view. Thus, I do not so much rush to judgment (critical or praising) as I might have in the past. There is an ease with which my senses take in both the overt occurrences being described and the more subliminal flow.

You will note, for instance, that Bert allows himself to go with a hunch sometimes, or to globalize an observation. If I were to move directly into pure opposition (the cozy place of my righteous indignation), or to the equally reflexive "other side," I might miss out on where he ultimately lands and why it is felt as healing for the client. So I invite you to stay present with everyone. This work is a process. It is a collaboration; dissonant, harmonizing, moving.

As to some of the landmarks on your map, the observations are subjective – any time we stop action for a moment to express what is being seen or felt or known in that moment is inherently subjective. It is the reader's collaboration, the hundreds of readers' engagement, that takes these observations out of the realm of subjectivity. It is an ongoing process that diffuses singularity and ignites shared clarity over time. And before time passes into that horizon, if we are present with everyone, we can imagine what it is that makes a movement or insight so healing. It is the more intriguing question, always.

You will at certain points see that your map is faulty, that where there was indicated a rocky pass ahead, actually the road is smooth. And other times when you were confident that the path was going to be level for a while, suddenly it becomes steep and challenging. Of course, this is the nature of the human landscape: we all (clients and guides) are complex beings. There are unforeseen circumstances, and shadowy memories. Bert calls upon his own guides along the way; sometimes he must listen right through his surprise, setting up the figures who strike him as pivotal and letting them go if they turn out not to be. Other times, he is simply a speaker, sharing reflections or "power sentences" that are in accord with next steps for the client.

Bert refers to a consciousness beyond the normal consciousness: he is alluding to mystical or supernatural fields, which include possession and past lives, and he is looking to the simpler phenomena of nonverbal communication, historical forces and intergenerational themes. The images, however, are most remarkable when they can be seen beyond the specificity of their passing nomenclature.

About 80 percent of this book is devoted to working with children across many contexts, in various ways. It has always been about the children anyway, the children and the future, being in accord with the elements of creativity, maintaining or attaining a generative stance, aligning with love.

There is a spectacular section in which we are privy to Bert's work with an entire learning community: young students, their families, teachers, and principals. And there is attention to children whose lives have been presumably disrupted for some reason and who are navigating adoption, foster care, and group homes.

It is amazing to feel into the environment as young people and children take their places beside Bert or in the constellations. Bert's love and tender honesty are forces that cut through the details of their current dilemmas.

In the last section of the book, which Bert calls "Mystic Consciousness," he returns to the fundamental questions that we carry throughout our lives around relationship, success, growing up, anxiety, loss … Always, Bert Hellinger is true to himself, fearless in following his road toward the horizon and opening his hand to anyone who wishes to accompany him.

An accidental companion, perhaps, it has never occurred to me that I had to understand the world exactly as Bert does. The invitation has always been to learn from what he has learned, and to come to myself not to him, to arrive. In that vast wide-open I have indeed received a lot, everything I need. The rest I can do. So I suppose that's really the map: to open your heart and mind to everything that is possible and nurture that courageousness by keeping your eyes open and allowing breath to all of your senses. Maybe fold the directions up, put them in your breast pocket, and listen for the sounds of life.

Suzi Tucker

Introduction

This book tells you stories, true stories. We can read them as stories through which we can look into our soul, into our own child-soul, and into the souls of our children. We can even read these stories to our children, but only one at a time. Older children can read the stories by themselves and gain a kind of understanding of their own souls that brings them a sense of relief. Finally they can see a way out for themselves, and the same goes for us, for us personally and for our children.

How do we read this book? Perhaps in a way that liberates us, taking us beyond our fears and our concerns to discover whether we and our children are on the right path.

We look into our soul and we breathe a sigh of relief. Opening up to these stories, letting them take us along, what is the result?

We comprehend: all children are good, and the same is true of us, provided we look into our soul with love.

PART ONE:
THE SOULS OF CHILDREN

Helping That Challenges

Recordings from a course for youth in homes and
for their caretakers and parents
Bad Kreuznach, 2001

Background

HELLINGER: Many children are burdened through various fates and childhood experiences, especially those who end up in a home outside of the one they were born into. Some of them lost one or both parents, others were given away, or there was not enough room at home -- whatever the reasons. These are oppressive fates. Some cope with their situation more easily, others find it more difficult. Quite often it is only the difficulty related to these immediate circumstances that we look at. These children look at the mother and the father, perhaps without even knowing them. But they look at them, and perhaps they feel anger towards them. They miss their parents, and they are sad, sometimes desperately so. If they remain in this kind of connection, the child to the parents, the parents to the child, tension builds up. The children cannot widen their gaze to their parents as they are.

Our parents as they are

What does it mean: parents and children? It means that the children have received their life from these parents. There are no other parents than these. Therefore they are the best parents, the only possible parents, and therefore also the only right parents.

The question is: Where does life come from, this life that our parents passed on to us? They got it from their parents, and on it goes down the line. Life comes from afar, and we cannot ever fathom this depth. It disappears into something we cannot recognize or grasp in any way.

And yet, life, as it flows through the generations, is always the same. There are no changes in passing life on. Therefore it makes no difference how the parents were. In what they received and then passed on, all of them are the same.

The wide-open heart

If children have a heavy fate, and yet they do not just look at the parents, but at the many generations down the line, all the way to the origin of life, if the children can take their life from there, as it came through all these generations, their hearts widen. We know and feel that beyond our parents we are embedded in something much larger and greater, and we also receive a special strength from this greater dimension.

Nevertheless, through these special parents we also experience ourselves as limited. We lack some opportunities on the one hand, and yet we are also given certain skills and options. A heavy fate is often greater than a light one. I will tell you a story about that.

Greatness

In London I worked with a woman who had polio. She sat in a wheelchair, with a loving husband by her side. I asked her: "Did your parents express their gratitude that everything went okay for you?"

As she shook her head, I asked her: "Can you make up for this now, that you give thanks for your life?" And she could do it.

Then I asked her to imagine that she grew up like other girls, and then I let her imagine how she grew up the way it really was. Afterwards I asked her: "What is greater?" That made her cry. I asked her again: "Which fate is greater, yours or the other one?" She replied: "Mine." Behind this statement was different power.

In this way, all those who have a special fate need to see that there is a special power behind them, once they agree and do something with it.

Here I will work with the youth in this sense. I will see if I can find a good solution. I will check if I can mobilize energies that are there through their parents, through their fate and their background, so that they can master their life with the support of this energy, so that they can feel: The life I have is right and good.

The ties

HELLINGER: I am a part of a family. Our family is embedded in something greater still, in a group, and it is guided by a shared conscience. This conscience is not conscious. It has hard and fast laws. The first draconic law in this conscience says: There must be no exclusion of anyone who belongs. If someone *is* excluded, this conscience will force a later-born member to represent the excluded person. So the individuals in a group are under the spell of this conscience, and therefore are not free.

Who belongs to our family?

Therefore we need to know who belongs to the family group that is ruled by this shared conscience. Beginning from below, we have the parents and their siblings, then the grandparents, sometimes also the great-grandparents. These are the blood relatives.

Then we have all those who had to leave the family, so that someone else could take their place. For instance, the father's first wife died, and thus made room for the second wife. So the first wife still belongs. This also applies if the father and the first wife are divorced. The first wife still belongs.

Where a family has great riches that they acquired at the expense of others, especially at the cost of their lives, the victims belong as well.

And something else is important, which I only began to see clearly in recent years: If there were murderers in the family, their victims also belong. Conversely, if there is a murdered victim in the family, the murderer also belongs to the family.

This has far-reaching consequences. In Israel for instance I could see that in the families of the Holocaust survivors the murderers of their family members belong as well. If this is not acknowledged, they are represented in these families. The murderers must be included. For us in Germany, this means that we must open our hearts to those we reject as criminals from the Nazi era, and give them a place amongst us. Or else there cannot be peace.

I had a constellation at the Ben Gurion University in Israel. It was a female client who was clearly suicidal. She wanted to follow her murdered family members. The blessing that allowed her to stay alive did not come from the victims. It came from the perpetrators. It shook her deeply to see this.

The other love

When we are dealing with children or youth, not knowing how to help them when they are perhaps recalcitrant or aggressive, or they want to take off or even die, we are sometimes tempted to give them good advice. The caretakers know this is completely useless, for the child or the youth does not feel understood.

Whatever they do, trying to kill themselves, running away, being aggressive, they all do it out of love. The question is though: For whom? We must find out where their love goes, and with whom they are angry perhaps, because they love them.

When we know that, we have new perspectives and new options. Then such a child feels understood, and the young person can begin to gather some strength for something greater. Therefore, what comes to light through family constellations is so valuable, all these entanglements, even generations back.

I'll give you an example of how something like this can unfold.

At a workshop in Japan, a woman said she did not want to go home because her parents rejected her. And then I took a representative for her mother and one for her. Her representative made an angry face. Then I asked her to say to her mother: "I'll kill you!" She said she didn't have the courage to say that.

Then I took the real client and placed her in the constellation and asked her to say the same thing to her mother: "I'll kill you!" She said it with rage. When I asked her if the sentence was correct, she said: "Not quite, I only want her to die."

And in real terms, it means that this woman wants to kill herself. Her soul can't bear this. When people have such aggressive feelings toward their parents, they kill themselves. There is no way out of that. But I did nothing. I broke off the constellation and didn't do anything with her any more.

I even forgot her. To forget her is a spiritual exercise. This way the clients are no longer influenced by me and they cannot express their feelings against me.

Towards the end of the course she came to me and said: "I can't find peace, there's something I really want to do." A colleague suggested doing an ancestors' line. I agreed.

I placed a representative for her mother, behind her one for the mother's mother, and so forth, until there were eight generations. Then I put the client in front of this ancestors' line, in order to see where the flow of love was disrupted.

The client turned to her mother, but from her mother there was no love flowing to the daughter. Then the mother turned around to her mother. Love did not flow there either. And so it went on down the line, until it reached the eighth mother. She had clenched fists, moved back a bit, and looked at the floor. One could see that there was a murder. To look at the floor often means to look at a dead person, and the clenched fists indicate a murder.

Then I asked a man to lie down in front of this mother. The client immediately crawled to this dead person and began to sob loudly, and she embraced him. She was identified with him, eight generations back. After I got both of them to stand again, placing the dead person next to his mother, she could turn to her daughter with love, and this daughter could turn to her daughter, until all mothers could turn to their daughters.

As soon as this dead person was acknowledged as belonging to the family, love flowed freely again amongst all these generations.

Afterwards the client crawled to her mother, knelt in front of her, embraced her feet, sobbed loudly, and said to her: "Dear Mummy!"

Interjection

PARTICIPANT: A little comment on the matter of the perpetrators and victims and your example from Israel. I feel there is something tragic and something comical. On the one hand, these people have been through Holocaust, and they are facing the Palestinians, and they incur guilt. Through the fact that they load guilt on themselves, they create a family connection with their victims, and what they really wanted to avoid, is happening. This is the comical aspect in this.

HELLINGER: You have no empathy with the Israelis.

PARTICIPANT: Yes, perhaps.

HELLINGER: Therefore you cannot solve anything either.

I had a constellation in Israel with a young man. His family traveled to Egypt with a group, and an Egyptian guard started shooting wildly and killed eight Israeli children, amongst them the client's sister, eight years old at the time. I set up the Israeli children who were shot, the Egyptian guard, and the client. The client did not want to look at them and he turned away. Nothing shifted in him. Then I got five representatives to lie down as the Palestinian children who were shot by the Israelis.

After this, movement began in the group. Some of the Israeli children wanted to go to the Palestinian children, but these children withdrew again.

Then I set up representatives for the parents of the Israeli children who were shot and also for the parents of the Palestinian children who were shot.

The Egyptian guard went to the parents and cried. The client turned to the parents on both sides, and they embraced. The Palestinian children crawled on the floor to reach the Israeli children.

Only when we look at everyone and give everyone a place in our heart can we begin to further peace, not before.

Questions about the example from Japan

PARTICIPANT: I have a question about the example from Japan that you recounted here, with the aggressive woman. If I do not have the capacity or opportunity to recognize that eight generations ago a murder took place, what options does this woman have to emerge from her aggression against her mother?

HELLINGER: None. This is entanglement.

PARTICIPANT: In earlier constellations I saw that the murderers were excluded. Has this been revised through recent insights, or does it only apply in some cases?

HELLINGER: When I began to do family constellations, it was clear that murderers have a bad influence on the other family members whilst they are amongst them. At that time I had not yet seen that they must be integrated into the family together with the victims. This is the new understanding.

More stories

I will tell you a few more stories for your orientation. In a workshop in Washington was a woman who had adopted a child. She was there with her partner. We set this up and found a solution.

The child's mother did not want this child, neither did the child's father. Therefore the woman and her partner had adopted the infant.

I took a representative for the birthmother and a representative for the biological father. I put seven generations of mothers behind the mother, and seven generations of fathers behind the father.

The adoptive mother had the adopted child with her, it was just a month old. She showed the child to each of the mothers behind the birth mother.

All of them looked kindly on the child, with the exception of the birthmother. But the grandmother, the great-grandmother, and all the other mothers looked kindly on the child. The child's adoptive father took the child in his arms and showed him to the line of fathers. They all looked kindly on the child.

Soon after the constellation I received a letter from this couple. The child had always wrinkled his forehead. After the constellation the baby's face lit up.

We do not just look at the biological parents, but far down the line, and we go to the earlier generations to receive the blessing and the strength we need.

Constellation with Kevin

Kevin is 16 years old, and for the last five years he has been living in a home, by his own choice. His mother died under circumstances yet unexplained; his father is a musician, who cannot bring him up due to his circumstances.

HELLINGER *to Kevin who is sitting next to him*: Close your eyes. Now something in you shifted and is now in motion. Allow it to express itself as it wishes. I let you have the full time.

HELLINGER *after a while*: Now withdraw slowly.

Kevin leans his head forward. Hellinger picks up on this deliberate movement, puts his arm around him, and with his other arm he holds his head, to draw it softly to his chest.

After a while, Hellinger gets a female representative to stand in front of what is happening. Kevin opens his eyes. He and the woman look at each other for a long time.

After a while, Kevin leans back in his chair, still looking at the woman.

HELLINGER *to Kevin*: Say to her: "Mama, I have everything."

KEVIN: Mama, I have everything.

HELLINGER: Look at her while you speak: "Mama, I have everything."

KEVIN: Mama, I have everything.

HELLINGER: "I will do something with it."

KEVIN: I will do something with it

HELLINGER: "You don't have to worry."

KEVIN: You don't have to worry.

HELLINGER: "You can have your peace now."

KEVIN: You can have your peace now.

Kevin is crying. Hellinger draws Kevin's head to his shoulder.

HELLINGER: Tell her: "I miss you very much."

KEVIN: I miss you very much.

HELLINGER: "In me you are still alive."

KEVIN: In me you are still alive.

11

HELLINGER: Look at her as you speak.

after a while: Tell her: "I will pass on what you gave me."

KEVIN: I will pass on what you gave me.

HELLINGER: "With love."

KEVIN: With love.

Hellinger gets a man to stand in front of what is happening.

HELLINGER *to Kevin*: This is your father. Say to him: "Now I give you up forever."

Kevin silently looks at his father for a long time.

HELLINGER *to Kevin*: Tell your father: "I have everything. Now I renounce you forever."

KEVIN: I have everything, I renounce everything.

HELLINGER: No. "I renounce you forever."

KEVIN: I renounce you forever.

HELLINGER: "But I have everything."

KEVIN: But I have everything.

HELLINGER: "Others helped me in your place."

KEVIN: Others helped me in your place.

HELLINGER: "Now I am strong enough."

KEVIN: Now I am strong enough.

Kevin looks at his father again, for a long time.

HELLINGER: Say to him: "Thanks for life"

KEVIN: Thanks for life.

HELLINGER: Say it a bit friendlier.

KEVIN: Thanks for life.

HELLINGER: "I'll do something with it."

KEVIN: I'll do something with it.

HELLINGER: "You don't have to worry about me any more."

KEVIN: You don't have to worry about me any more.

HELLINGER: "I renounce you forever."

KEVIN: I renounce you forever.

HELLINGER: Now you just sit up like someone who is strong. Yes, like that. Upright inside, yes, that's it, exactly.

There's a story in the Bible. There was man who had five talents, and he didn't do anything with them. Another man had only one talent, and he overtook all the others. He did something with it.

I'll tell you one more story. A man was in a train in the sleeper coach. He slept in the lower berth, and another man was lying in the upper berth. The one in the upper berth kept on saying: "I am so hungry, I am so hungry." The one below went to the restaurant car and got something to eat for the other man.

After a while the one in the upper berth started again: "I was so hungry, I was so hungry."

Okay? Well, that's it.

HELLINGER *as a caretaker talks to Kevin and embraces him*: When someone has worked with me like this, then he is strong. Nobody must attend to him and nobody must ask: "Well how was that?"

This is a brutal interference in someone else's soul. Such inquirers are curious, they draw energy away from him, into their own soul. This is serious. Kevin has everything. He has his parents, and he knows what he is doing.

To Kevin: All the best to you.

Being a victim

HELLINGER: I did many therapies over many years, and I found out there is only one thing that matters, something quite straightforward.

Therapy knows only one path that leads to success: We connect the person with the father and mother. That's all. Some have less of a struggle doing it, others have more. Some remain stuck in reproaches of their parents.

We can't work with people who present as victims. As long as people present as victims, they are aggressive towards others. Those towards whom they present themselves in this way get angry. When they go to a therapist, they make the therapist angry: "I am so poor, you must help me. And don't you dare not help me the way I want you to." This is the aggression in presenting as a victim.

Many who were in a home (for troubled teens, or foster care, etc.) have complaints against their parents: "If it had been different, I would have turned out different." That's the belief.

Some years ago a hypnotherapist from America did an exercise with a group I participated in. He placed three rectangles on the floor next to each other. One stood for the ideal parents. Standing on that rectangle, we have the ideal parents. The question is, how does it feel?

Then we stand on the next rectangle. It stands for the worst possible parents. On the third rectangle we look at our parents as they really are.

What was the result? How does it feel? It feels the same on each one of them.

Many who were in homes, or children who were adopted out, feel a calling to complain to others. They present as victims, to claim pity. But there are those who can say: "This is how my parents were, and that is okay with me. I received everything I need; others stepped in to help me on, and now I will do something with it." Through this attitude they are free, and they look to the future.

14

I'll take you to your father

HELLINGER: Now I will continue. You are a family? Come over here. Which one of you is the problem now?

WOMAN: After what I heard here, I've been thinking hard, which one of us is the real problem.

HELLINGER: Quite obvious, the problem is with you. Your son, the poor boy, is the one who has to carry it.

To the group: Did you see how she put the burden on him? Instead of looking at me, she looked at him.

To the woman: Do you have several children?

WOMAN: Yes.

HELLINGER: How many?

WOMAN: Three.

HELLINGER: Were you married before?

WOMAN: Yes.

HELLINGER: From which marriage is he? Or are there some other connections?

WOMAN: There are other connections. This happened between my two marriages.

HELLINGER: So he is in between. Do you have children from the first marriage?

WOMAN: Yes.

HELLINGER: How many?

WOMAN: One.

HELLINGER: And then it's this son, and then you have one more child?

WOMAN: Then I have a child with my present husband.

HELLINGER: And this one here is your present husband? Okay. And what about this boy's father?

WOMAN: No idea.

HELLINGER: What do you mean, no idea?

WOMAN: I don't know how he's doing, what he is up to. He just left.

HELLINGER: Are you angry with him?

WOMAN: Not any more.

HELLINGER: We heard it in your voice that you are still angry with him.

WOMAN: If I am still angry with him, I am not aware of it.

HELLINGER: If you are or were angry with him, whatever, you are angry at the part of your son that takes after his father. Do you know who has a place in my heart?

WOMAN: No idea.

HELLINGER: With me, his father has a place in my heart. That's why your son likes me.

A constellation follows where this son is standing opposite his father.

HELLINGER *to the son:* Look at him. I'm not important, he is important. Say to him: "Please look at me."

SON: Please look at me.

HELLINGER: "I'm your son after all."

SON: I'm your son after all.

HELLINGER: Look at your mother and say to her: "Please look at him."

SON: Please look at him.

HELLINGER: "He's my father after all."

SON: He's my father after all.

HELLINGER *as he sees that she wants to go closer to the son's father:* Go with your movement.

The woman goes towards him slowly.

HELLINGER: Tell him: "I loved you."

WOMAN: I loved you.

HELLINGER: Go a little closer. Tell him: "I was very upset with you."

WOMAN: I was very upset with you.

HELLINGER *as he sees that the boy wants to move:* Go with the movement as you want to move.

The son begins to sway.

HELLINGER *to the son:* Fall down, fall down.

The son falls down.

HELLINGER: This is the effect of a curse from his mother. It knocks the child to the floor.

To the woman: There is only one thing that will help the boy. You must tell him: "I will take you to your father."

WOMAN: I will take you to your father.

HELLINGER *to the group:* I will tell you a little story about this. A female psychoanalyst had two sons with her husband. They were separated, and she said: "Their father doesn't do anything with the children."

I asked her: "Do you have any respect for him?" She said: "No." I said: "Exactly, that's why he does not do anything with the children."

Two years later I met her again and I asked: "How are you?" She said: "Their father took the children for a holiday." This is the beginning of the solution. Back to the first love, give it room again, no matter what happened. Only then can the child be well again.

The rejected parent is a big loss for the child, a big loss. Here the son was knocked down to the floor. We have seen how the son went backwards because the mother went backwards instead of forwards.

I would like to say something to the mother. When someone is angry, then sometimes I get this person to say the following sentence: What on earth have *I* done to you that I am so angry with you? It is often the very opposite to what it appears to be. From her reaction here this is likely to be the case. The father was very moved and full of love.

I break this off here, I think we have seen what was essential here.

to the son: You can say to your mother: "All the love you show to my stepfather is no replacement for this love." But your stepfather has looked after you all this time, quite obviously so. Give him a big place in your heart for this, side by side with your father. He will get a big place in your heart, of course.

Meditation

HELLINGER *to the group*: I will do a little exercise with you. You can close your eyes. Now you can scan your life and see before you the people with whom you are angry. They all stand next to each other, those who hurt you, and those whom you hurt. Then you go to each one of them. You look into the eyes of the first one and you say: "I am like you, exactly like you." You feel what this does to your soul, when you say this. Then you go to the next one: "I am like you, you are like me." Then to the next one. You look into this person's eyes and you open your heart: "I am like you, you are like me."

When you have met everyone in your line, you turn towards the horizon, all together. It is still dark, and the light is hidden. Before this hidden light you bow together.

I will tell you another story. A while ago when I was in Israel, I went to Lake Genezareth. This is the place where Jesus gave the Sermon on the Mount. A marvelous place, so quiet, so peaceful.

It was there that Jesus said: "Blessed are those who bring peace, for they shall be called the children of God." And he said: "Love your enemies. Do good to those who hate you. For my heavenly father also lets the sun shine over the righteous and the unjust, and he lets the rain fall on the good and on the bad." We all know that.

As we drove back, I pondered: What goes on in a soul that opens up to this? What exactly does this mean? If we feel our way into this soul, if we succeed in that, what must be happening inside then?

At that moment a sentence came to me: Love means, acknowledging that all others are the same as me before something greater. Acknowledging that all others are just like me before something greater.

Humility is the same. Forgiving and forgetting as well. Acknowledging that all others are the same as me in front of something greater. Well that was a little addition to this constellation. All the best to you.

The caretakers

I would like to say something to the caretakers in homes. If they help too much, the child gets angry with them. The caretakers help with a little distance, above all they help as the representatives of the parents. It matters that the caretakers take up a place below the parents. When they want to be bigger, as if they were the better parents, the children get angry.

This morning we could see this so beautifully in that one constellation. The father of the child stood behind the home. On the one hand, he had wiggled out of his responsibility, on the other, he stood behind the home. The home could lean on him. This was helpful and beautiful. When the help for the children is given to them in this sense, composed and in harmony with the parents, and if these children are allowed to become like their parents, they feel safe. Children want to become like their parents.

When someone says: "Your father is an alcoholic," then out of loyalty the child will become just like him. This is the effect that such outer influences have on the child's soul. The child will become like the father. The child says: "I want to be like you." Then the father looks lovingly at the child and says: "You can also do things a bit differently than I have." This frees the child to develop outside the sphere of the parents.

Here, too, it is always the same. I have thought about what makes a human being great. Everything that makes us the same as others makes us great. Everything that deviates from the sameness with others makes us smaller. This greatness is a humble greatness. With this greatness we can move calmly and easily amongst all humans. As soon as people make themselves bigger than others, others don't want them. This making oneself bigger than others produces aggression, and this also works in the other direction. Those who behave like equals among equals are welcome anywhere, no matter where they go.

Me for you

HELLINGER: Okay, let's continue with our work. Who wants to?
To a home resident who is already an adult before the law: Do you want to have your turn now?
HELLINGER *as she nods*: Do you know your parents?
CLIENT: Yes, both of them, my mother and my father.
HELLINGER: Where do they come from?

CLIENT: My father is American, from Alabama, and my mother is German.

HELLINGER: How is the relationship between your parents?

CLIENT: Pretty good, really.

HELLINGER: Nice. Are they together?

CLIENT: Yes.

HELLINGER: Why did you end up in a home?

CLIENT: Because I could not get on with my father any more.

HELLINGER: Did you oppose him?

CLIENT: Yes, I saw no other way any longer.

HELLINGER: Who else was angry with him?

CLIENT: Angry how?

HELLINGER: I'm just asking generally.

CLIENT: I did not get on with my father. I don't know why, either.

HELLINGER: Do you have siblings?

CLIENT: Yes, a sister.

HELLINGER: Older or younger?

CLIENT: Older.

HELLINGER: Was one of your parents in another relationship before?

CLIENT: My father was married before.

HELLINGER: This other woman, what is she like?

CLIENT: I did not know her.

HELLINGER: What is she like? What does one say about her?

CLIENT: That she is from Thailand.

HELLINGER: So she was a Thai woman? Your father travels around the whole world?

CLIENT: No, he was a soldier in Vietnam. Then he was also on a holiday, or stationed elsewhere. I'm not sure.

HELLINGER: Okay, let's have a look at what we can do for you. I will set up two people. You already know whom I want to set up, don't you? I'm always an ally of the people who are excluded, you see. Who is excluded here?

CLIENT: No idea.

HELLINGER: The Thai woman is excluded. My guess is that she is angry with your father. You represent her. That's why you had altercations with your father. Not because you have issues with him, but because she has issues with him. You are identified with her. This is my image. Of course, now I will have to put it to the test. Okay? Well then.

In addition to the client, Hellinger chooses a man as her father's representative and a woman for the Thai wife.

HELLINGER *to the representatives*: I completely rely on you to go exactly with what goes on in your soul.

The constellation begins.

HELLINGER *to the young client in response to what showed up in the constellation*: Your father isn't exactly friendly to her. Do you know the meaning of what we see in the constellation? He had choked her.

HELLINGER *to the group*: The Thai woman hides behind her, and the client takes on her aggression. We can see her clenched fists. What the first wife suppressed, is taken on by her.

HELLINGER *after a while, to the client*: Tell her: "I avenge you."

CLIENT: I avenge you.

HELLINGER: "I am the big one here."

CLIENT: I am the big one here.

HELLINGER: "And you are only the little one."

CLIENT: And you are only the little one.

HELLINGER: "You poor Thai sausage."

CLIENT: You poor Thai sausage.

HELLINGER: "I can do it better."

CLIENT: I can do it better.

HELLINGER *after a while:* Now get on your knees and tell her: "You are the big one here."

CLIENT: You are the big one here.

HELLINGER: "And I'm the little one."

CLIENT: And I'm the little one.

Hellinger chooses a representative for the mother of the young client and places her in the constellation.

HELLINGER *to the client:* Tell your father: "She is my mother."

CLIENT: She is my mother.

HELLINGER: "She is the only right one for me."

CLIENT: She is the only right one for me.

HELLINGER: "I have nothing to do with your other wife."

CLIENT: I have nothing to do with your other wife.

HELLINGER: "I am only the child here."

CLIENT: I am only the child here.

HELLINGER: "Please look at me as your daughter."

CLIENT: Please look at me as your daughter.

HELLINGER: "And take me as your child."

CLIENT: And take me as your child.

HELLINGER: Say this to your mother as well.

CLIENT *to her mother's representative:* "Look at me as your child and take me as your child."

HELLINGER *chooses three men after a while:* I take the three of you; lie down on the floor here, with your head in this direction, a little further away.

To the group: These are the Vietnamese from the war.

To the client: Look at them.

HELLINGER *after a while:* Tell your father: "Please look at them."

CLIENT: Please look at them.

HELLINGER *after a while, again to her:* Go down to the dead, go down, go down to the dead.

HELLINGER *after a while, to the father:* Tell her: "I'll take this on."

FATHER: I will deal with this.

HELLINGER: "This is none of your business."

FATHER: This is none of your business.

HELLINGER *after a while to the father:* Lie down next to them. *To the child:* And you get up, and the mother as well. And the two of you bow to them.

HELLINGER *to the child,* Say: "Dear Daddy."

CLIENT: Dear Daddy.

HELLINGER: "Please look kindly at me if I stay alive."

CLIENT: Please look kindly at me if I stay alive.

HELLINGER *after a while:* How is this for the father?

The father has no response.

HELLINGER *to the father:* Say to your daughter: "I can't be friendly any more."

FATHER: I can't be friendly any more.

HELLINGER: "The guilt is too big."

FATHER: The guilt is too big.

HELLINGER: "But I want you to live."

FATHER: But I want you to live.

HELLINGER *to the child:* Now turn around, the mother as well, turn around, both of you.

CLIENT: I am trying to go further because I can see that my mother is just like my father.

HELLINGER *to the client:* Lie down with them, on your back.

After a while: Is this better or worse?

CLIENT: Better.

HELLINGER: Exactly. Now get up, look at your father and say to him: "I will die so that you can live."

CLIENT: I will die so that you can live.

HELLINGER: "I'll carry it for you."

CLIENT: I'll carry it for you.

HELLINGER *after a while*: How is this for the father?

FATHER: This is wrong.

HELLINGER: Tell her: "This is none of your business."

FATHER: This is none of your business. It's up to me what I am doing.

HELLINGER: Tell her: "Get out of here."

FATHER: Get out of here.

HELLINGER *to the client*: Now you can go forward.

After a while: Okay, you can stop there, it's far enough.

HELLINGER *to the client*: How are you now?

CLIENT: A bit better.

HELLINGER *to the representatives*: The dead shall get up now, and the Thai woman also. You all stand behind her, one after the other.

To the client: Lean into them, yes, like this. Close your eyes and breathe deeply. This is where the blessing comes from – and now it also comes from your father.

HELLINGER *after a while to the client:* How are you now?

CLIENT: Better.

HELLINGER: Okay, that's it. Thank you all.

To the father's representative: And to you especially. Now I will show you how you will become yourself.

Imagine her father in front of you and bow to him, quite lightly. Then you turn away again. Okay, you did that well.

To the group: This was a good example to experience that all people are the same. Now we have arrived at large-scale politics. Perhaps you can look at what I said earlier about the distinction between good and bad, or rather about the nondistinction between good and bad. We are all embedded in something that we cannot escape from. Let this pass through your soul again. And also what I said about the love of children. Here it is clear, and we can see this quite often: In families where the father was in a war, involved in war, the victims also belong to the family.

There was a man from the US, a bit of a scallywag. He said his father was a hero. He was involved in conquering the island of Iwo Jima. He was in a unit that raised the American flag after heavy losses.

I set up the father's mates who died on the island in that battle. And I set up five representatives for the victims of Iwo Jima, victims of the Americans. The son was drawn to them. The father was quite frozen - but the son was irresistibly drawn to them. I could not help him. Then I placed the son in front of his father and told him to say: "I will go to them. I don't care what happens to you." This is what he said. This is how much he was connected to his father's dead companions.

Only as the father looked deeply into his son's eyes, and began to realize what he had caused through his stiffness in the face of the dead, did he begin to soften. Then he could honor the dead, and slowly withdraw from them, together with his son. Something similar we could see here as well.

To the child: Your heart is not with the Thai woman, but with these dead. You represent them in your family. But they must be with your father, and your father with them. You are too small here, far too small.

In this context I would like to say something else: the family conscience follows the law that all who belong must belong.

Therefore in this conscience there is no distinction between good and bad.

Another law is at work here. It says: Those who came earlier have precedence over those who came later. Someone who was born later must not interfere in something that earlier ones have done. If they try regardless, they will fail. Whatever you will do if you want to kill yourself to atone for your father, it will be in vain. It does not help anyone. But you may have the feeling that you are great and innocent. Every failing hero feels great. But afterwards he is lying slain among the dead. What did all his greatness achieve?

You know a bit of English. In one of Shakespeare's plays there is Falstaff, the big fat one, a comical figure. He was supposed to go to war, but he wiggled out of it and stayed behind. He was a coward. Because he was a coward, he survived. One of the great ones who had fought in full fervor lay slain, and they buried him. Falstaff said: "Thus heroism comes to an end. But I as the coward live on." So you can die heroically or live cowardly. Or more precisely, you can live with a guilty conscience or die with a clear conscience. If you do the dying for your father, you feel innocent; if you stay alive, you will perhaps feel a little guilty. We can only survive with guilt. Have I clarified this for you? Okay, then go and live.

The good conscience

PARTICIPANT: Why should one forgive the enemy?

HELLINGER: One does not forgive the enemy.

PARTICIPANT: Did you not say that this morning?

HELLINGER: One becomes like the enemy.

PARTICIPANT: What does this mean?

HELLINGER: We become the same as our enemies. Then we have no need to forgive them. We acknowledge that we are the same.

Good and bad

Perhaps in this connection I can explain something about good and bad. It looks like this is something that occupies you, good and bad.

The question is: Is there anything good? Is there anything bad? No, it does not exist. But we use this distinction for our daily life, to give us an orientation. The distinction between good and bad comes about through our conscience. If we have a clear conscience, we say we did something good. If we have a bad conscience, we say we did something bad.

Good and bad in this connection only means: good is that which helps me to belong to my family, and bad is what threatens my belonging. Therefore, our conscience helps us to make the distinction between what we must do and must not do in order to belong. This is the task of our conscience. So, this is where the distinction of good and bad exists.

Families are all different. What counts as good in one family is scorned by another. And vice versa. Therefore people from another family may act badly according to the ideas that my family upholds, and they do it with a good conscience. Therefore children in group homes may act in ways that are seen as impossible in familial homes, with a good conscience.

Therefore we can't appeal to their conscience. It does not help. Once we know what is seen as good in their family, then we can talk to them from the perception their family has in terms of good conscience. This helps. This is the difference here.

There are things that are bad. For instance, if someone kills another person, of course that is terrible. Or what goes on in wars, all that is terrible. Yet this is so from our perspective, from our distinction between good and bad.

Now it is so that we also transfer our conscience and the distinction between good and bad to God. We think that God judges over heaven and hell according to our conscience. This is our assumption. Therefore, seen from the perspective of the US, the terrorists who attacked the World Trade Center will be sent to hell by God, and they help to make sure this happens.

Conversely, the terrorists have the same ideas about the US. They want God to send them to hell, and they assist God to make sure it happens. So both sides are caught in their respective consciences. Thus what is orchestrated by fate or by something greater defies the assessment of our own conscience. What we experience as dangerous or unpleasant, or as despicable or worthy of rejection, is only so according to our conscience. In the eyes of a greater power it serves another purpose.

An old friend of mine, who died a long time ago, around 475 BC, said: *War is the father of all things*. Without conflict there is no progress. Imagine there was nothing "bad" left. We would sit around with fat bellies and do nothing. What a dreadful thing.

And the things that happen now, in different kinds of wars, as terrible as the situations are for those caught up in them, are blessings for the world. All must find new ways of orientation, they must form new alliances, they must be involved with more different people than in the past. Even where we take sides for one and against another, after a while it turns out that everything serves a greater purpose. And the power who is in charge of all this is not merciful in the way we understand it. It challenges us.

Therefore we must also see the perpetrators as being in the service of another power. All perpetrators are conscientious. Your uncles (*to a participant*) were conscientious in killing that man. And those who executed your uncles also did it with a good conscience. They all acted out of their own good conscience, and therefore we have trouble making distinctions here.

In the end we are all the same before this greater power, and we might as well forget these distinctions between good and bad. Only when we are willing to look at these greater dimensions can we contribute to peace, can we understand others. Above all, we can understand children in their special ways of behaving. We entrust them to this greater power. This is a way of relating to them.

The Israeli about whom I told you this morning, whose sister was shot, he was unable to achieve an inner separation from her. He was still under the shock of the event and he was in danger of following his sister. I did an exercise with him, and in the end he was able to take his dead sister into his arms. He looked at her with love, as she is, no longer among the living. She is dead. He puts her into God's arms, so to speak. Then he steps back, and he leaves her there. We can do this with those we see as bad. This is called loving your enemy. This is something completely different from a commandment. It is an insight: basically, we are all the same.

Help for an autistic sister

HELLINGER *to three sisters*: Now I will work with the three of you. Come over here. What is it about?

FIRST SISTER: We are three of five sisters. Our youngest sister is autistic. She has been in a group home since she was 7. We feel as if she was pushed out, and we are at odds with that.

SECOND SISTER: We also have problems with our parents.

HELLINGER: Yes, I know, I was about to set up the parents.

Hellinger chooses representatives for the parents, for the autistic sister, for the absent sister, and he asks the three sisters who are present to represent themselves in the constellation. He asks the oldest sister to set up the constellation. In the constellation the mother looks outside and to the floor.

HELLINGER *after a while*: From the constellation one thing is quite clear: The mother is looking at a dead person.

He chooses a woman as the representative for this dead person and asks her to lie in front of the mother, with her back turned towards the mother.

HELLINGER *after a while to the autistic sister*: Go with the movement as it wants to be.

The autistic sister staggers, then goes down to the floor and lies in front of the father, away from the others.

HELLINGER: Go with your movement, just go down, just go down.
to the first sister: Do you know who the dead person in front of your mother is?

FIRST SISTER: My mother has two dead siblings, twins who died at birth.

Hellinger chooses still another woman and asks her to lie next to the first dead person. The mother kneels in front of her. Afterwards Hellinger asks the autistic sister to lie next to this dead woman. In the meantime the father has turned to the dead on the floor and to the autistic child. Soon the autistic child sits up.

HELLINGER *after a while to the mother*: Tell your autistic child: "My two sisters have a place in my heart."
MOTHER: My two sisters have a place in my heart.
HELLINGER: "Now they have a place."
MOTHER: Now they have a place.

Hellinger asks the three sisters to move to the side somewhat, next to the father, who had also moved farther away. They are all looking to the mother and to the dead. The autistic sister is now sitting up. One of the mother's sisters wants to stroke her, but the autistic child shakes her head.

In time Hellinger asks the mother to lie next to the dead. Then he asks the autistic sister to stand in front of the father, and then to go to her sisters. Then he places the father in front of his five daughters, who are in a row according to their age.

After a while Hellinger chooses a woman as the representative for the group home, and he places her to the right of the father, at a little distance.

The home slowly moves towards the autistic sister. Suddenly this sister throws her hands over her head and lets out a loud scream. Then her hands sink down.

HELLINGER: This was breaking free from the autism.
To the first sister: But there is something else, this alone is not enough. Do you know what it is?
FIRST SISTER: Our father's brother died from starvation, on the run from Pomerania, during the war. He was 1 ½ years old.
HELLINGER: Your father's brother?
FIRST SISTER: Yes.

Hellinger chooses a representative for the father's brother and gets him to stand to the right of the father. The father softy puts his arm around him. Then Hellinger asks the autistic sister to also go to the father's dead brother. She slowly goes towards him and takes him into her arms and holds him close. At first he has collapsed in on himself, but then he straightens up. The autistic sister holds him by the hand and looks into his eyes.

After a while Hellinger takes the autistic sister and gets her to stand with her sisters. The father's brother who died early turns to him. They look at each other with deep love.

Now Hellinger sets up the order of the family, the father's dead brother to the right of father, the mother with her dead sisters to the left of her husband, the sisters opposite their parents in order of age. Then he asks the representative of the home to sit down.

HELLINGER *to the autistic sister*: How is it now?
AUTISTC SISTER: Better, but I still have a lot of pressure here on my chest. I am not quite as confused as I was before.
HELLINGER *to the sisters*: Form a circle and put your arms around each other, all of you.

They embrace tenderly, their heads close together, and after a while they begin to laugh loudly, above all the sister who was autistic.

HELLINGER *after a while*: Five sisters! Okay, that's it!
to the group: Strange how much is at work in the depth, and how little progress we make when we only look at the surface. But a family constellation brings it to light, step by step.

What is essential in dealing with these matters is that our gaze widens. So we do not just look at what is obvious, but also at what is behind it. How strongly this still affects us, and how alive the dead are.

Questions

PARTICIPANT: When there was this screaming before, it was said, this is the way out of autism. This means, the child could get well again?
HELLINGER: With me, one needs to listen carefully. I said, this is the breaking out of the autism. We could see that. What is really happening I don't know. If we ask, like you just did, will that really help, then what is going on in your soul? Are you in accord, or is the accord broken?

PARTICIPANT: When I ask I am not in accord.

HELLINGER: Exactly. Yet the question does not only have an effect on your soul, but also on the system. Curious questions interfere with the movements of the soul. Therefore our reticence is necessary, total reticence.

I would also be happy to hear how she is doing, I held her in my heart. But I do not dare ask.

Whenever we want to achieve a particular result, in psychotherapy or in social work, or in group homes, as soon as a special goal is set, it will not work. It will always go wrong, because I put myself in the place of something bigger, perhaps trying to speed something up or to force something, and in that moment I am out of touch with what is greater.

What directs us, this greater soul, has greater things in mind than we do. When we entrust ourselves to it, we achieve far greater things.

Plans

Imagine I had made plans about what I want to do today, how much would I have achieved? Nothing, nothing at all. It only works in unison. Therefore it was important that you asked this question, so that we can hold ourselves to account for what happens through these little things that we take for granted, for instance through inquiring how things are going. In psychotherapy and in group homes many ask: What happened? Why this and why that? This inquisitiveness disturbs the movements of the soul. In contrast to this, if we are just present, in unison with the greater, this radiates forth immediately. This contains an incredible power. In Chinese philosophy we would refer to this as being active through non-action.

I always withdraw each time. Suddenly, when I have withdrawn this way, a sentence, or the next step, comes to me. Then I say or do

34

this, but I don't know where it will take us. Then again I wait for a little while. In this way, it unfolds step by step. We can never guess what might happen.

See it before you, with your inner eye: Just like the representatives perceive immediately what is happening in the family, the same way the family also perceives what goes on here. The solutions we are finding here have their effect on the family.

Curiosity

There is a story from Cologne. Once upon a time there were little helpful gnomes called Heinzelmännchen. They worked beautifully for a long time, at night when everyone was asleep, undetected - until a woman wanted to know who they were. That was the end of it. This is a fine example. The same applies here, too. Our utter reticence is full of respect. This respect lends wings to something in our soul. It opens an unknown space. But when a question comes, something shrinks in the soul, wondering what the other person has in mind. But nobody asks what the sun has in mind for us. The sun just shines. And just like this I let it shine on me, too.

Suicidal daughter

HELLINGER: A family from Berlin is sitting next to me now. The parents are both Polish. They are here because of their daughter. But I am not working with the daughter, first I will work with the mother. Then I will see what comes up. I had talked with her before, and she has told me a number of things.

There is a famous holy man, Vincent de Paul is his name. He founded Caritas and helped many people. He said to a friend: When someone wants to help you, be careful. Often we weaken someone if we want to help. Your daughter is a strong girl, I have seen that. She is stubborn, for instance. Okay, we just leave her be with herself for now, and I will work with the mother.

When I talked with her before, she told me a few things. Two uncles fought against the communists. People say that these two murdered one communist, and later on they were executed.

The question is now: Who does the daughter imitate? My image: the man who was murdered by the uncles. I will check this now. So we need two representatives for the uncles, I place them over here. To begin with, I'll do nothing, just observing what goes on in them.

The representatives for the uncles look to the floor, and they lean back, as if they want to leave. Hellinger chooses another man and gets him to lie down in front of them, on his back.

The uncles become restless, and they are drawn to the murdered man. One of them gets on his knees, without coming closer, and he keeps on looking to the floor. The other one looks at the murdered man's face for a long time, and finally he kneels down by his side.

After a time, Hellinger chooses a representative for the daughter and asks her to stand in the constellation as well. She slowly bends down to the murdered man. Hellinger asks her to lie down next to him. She lies down and looks across to him.

The second uncle lies down next to the murdered man. The first uncle has straightened up and he touches the murdered man with one hand.

HELLINGER *after a while:* Now the dead man has closed his eyes. *To the daughter's representative:* Now you get up.
HELLINGER: How was it for you when you were lying down, better or worse?
DAUGHTER'S REPRESENTATIVE: Better, I really wanted to look at the murdered man, but he did not want to look at me.

HELLINGER: The others were the important ones.

To the daughter: The dead man is excluded from the family, but he belongs to this family. The family has ignored him. Therefore you are suicidal. You said inside: "I will die in your place." These are the dynamics here. What do you say to that?

DAUGHTER: Well, I don't think I wanted to die in the place of my mother, but I just don't like the world. This is the reason.

HELLINGER *to the daughter's representative*: You can sit down now.

To the other representatives: You can get up now.

HELLINGER *to the murdered man*: How did you feel down there?

MURDERED MAN: Sometimes I had the feeling as if I had to cry.

HELLINGER: Exactly, this is how it is. They murdered you, and nobody looked at you. None of them looked at you, you felt that correctly. You did it well right from the start. In such a constellation the representatives feel like the real persons. This is the secret here.

HELLINGER *to one of the perpetrators*: How did you fare?

FIRST UNCLE: Cold, I was stiff and cold.

HELLINGER: *to the group*: He is not released yet. We can't do anything for him as yet.

To the second perpetrator: How was it for you?

SECOND UNCLE: In the beginning I was very shaky, but I had to look at him the whole time. I wanted to move closer to him, but I had the feeling as if I had lumps of concrete on my feet. I could only move towards him very slowly, and when he looked at me, it was a big relief. When I bent over him and looked at him, there was this helplessness again. When the woman came, I concentrated on her. Then there was a calmness again.

HELLINGER: So, when the daughter, even though she was not entitled to do this, did this anyway, she took that load off him.

Hellinger places the first uncle behind the second one, and the murdered man next to the right side of the second uncle. The daughter gets to stand in front of the murdered man and the second uncle, leaning into them backwards.

HELLINGER *to the daughter*: Close your eyes.

To the murdered man and the second uncle: You both put one hand on her shoulder.

To the daughter: Now you let the energy of the perpetrators, the murderers, and of the murdered man, flow into a union in you. Just close your eyes and take your time.

To the group: You can see, she's identified with the victim. The way she droops her head shows it. She must take the perpetrators into her soul, as human beings.

To the daughter: Breathe deeply with your mouth open, then it is easier for you.

To the representatives of the uncles and the murdered man: And you also look at each other at the same time. This helps her, too, when the perpetrators have a place in the heart of the victim, and the victim has a place in the heart of the perpetrators, from human being to human being.

HELLINGER *after a while to the daughter*: Now you turn around, and you turn to them and you put your arms around them, and you men put your arms around her. And breathe deeply.

To the uncles: And you imagine that the murdered man blesses her, with all good wishes for her, that she may be well.

After a while, to the daughter: Now you stand back a little, and you look at them. Look at them and bow to them, just very lightly. Now you look at them and you say: "You have a place in my heart, all of you."

DAUGHTER: You have a place in my heart, all of you.

HELLINGER: Look at them as you say it.

DAUGHTER: You have a place in my heart, all of you.

HELLINGER *after a while to the victim*: How does this feel for you?

MURDERED MAN: Good.

HELLINGER *to the daughter*: Now you can turn around, and turn away.

She turns around and looks ahead.

HELLINGER: Do you know what is there in front of you?

DAUGHTER: No, I don't know.

HELLINGER: Life. Right in front of you is life. Take a step forward, another one, another one…

She is still drooping her head. Hellinger touches her head and moves it into an upright position. He holds her head like this for a long time.

HELLINGER *to the daughter:* Now you can take your head out of the noose quite easily, and look ahead. Okay, I leave it here. Thank you all.

Adopted children

HELLINGER *to Viola*: Now I continue the work, with you. Shall I? You have seen so much already, so you can take heart that I will handle everything carefully.

Hellinger places representatives for her parents.

To Viola: Just close your eyes.

After a while: Close your eyes. Say to your mother: "Mummy, I let you go."

VIOLA: Mummy, I let you go.

HELLINGER: "Now I let you go."

VIOLA: Now I let you go.

HELLINGER: "You gave me away forever."

VIOLA: You gave me away forever.

HELLINGER: "Now I agree to it."

VIOLA: Now I agree to it.

HELLINGER: "Now I give you up forever."

VIOLA: Now I give you up forever.

HELLINGER: "But thank you for my life."

VIOLA: But thank you for my life.

HELLINGER: "Thank you for touching me."

VIOLA: Thank you for touching me.

HELLINGER: Tell her: "I am the little one here."

VIOLA: I am the little one here.

HELLINGER: "And you're the big one."

VIOLA: And you're the big one.

HELLINGER: "I remain the little one."

VIOLA: I remain the little one.

HELLINGER *after a while*: Look at your father and say to him: "You abandoned me."

VIOLA: You abandoned me.

HELLINGER: "Now I give you up forever."

VIOLA: Now I give you up forever.

HELLINGER: "Others kept me alive."

VIOLA: Others kept me alive.

HELLINGER: "Now I turn to them."

VIOLA: Now I turn to them.

HELLINGER: "But thanks for life."

VIOLA: But thanks for life.

HELLINGER: "Thank you for touching me."

VIOLA: Thank you for touching me.

HELLINGER *after a while*: How are you now?

VIOLA: Better.

HELLINGER: This has caused great pain of course, but now you emerge strengthened. *To the representatives of the parents*: Thank you both.

HELLINGER *to the group*: The information I had was: She is adopted and does not know her parents.

To Viola: Is this so?

VIOLA: Yes it is.

What do we have to keep in mind about adoptions?

HELLINGER: I heard that there are several participants from governmental youth services. Perhaps I should say something about adoptions and how we deal with them.

The first thing is: No mercy with the parents. This is the first thing. No mercy for the poor mother, even if she is only 14 years old, but mercy for the child. This is the first thing. Don't twist the situation upside down, that the big ones can play the little ones, and the little ones who can't defend themselves, end up having to carry the lot. Then the helpers are strengthened, then they have the right order in their soul.

The second thing is, that some have the idea that one could put something into order for the child, as if the child could find a way back to the parents, and they would take their child in. The child above all often has this hope. The parents won't do it.

Imagine: The parents gave the child up for adoption. They wanted to get rid of the child – and that is, for good. If the child comes to them later on, how will they respond? With guilt, of course. There is no chance for coming back together. This cannot be undone. Giving a child up forever cannot be reconciled and undone.

For the child it is important that he or she agrees to how it was. The parents gave the child away, forever. An adoption is like an abortion; we can compare the two. Therefore the child must say: Yes, I agree, and I give you up forever. This is painful. Then the child gains strength.

To Viola: But nevertheless you received life from them. They must have been beautiful parents. You have everything; the essential things you have received. But you could only stay alive through the adoptive parents, and you can stay close to them, with real love. They have kept you alive.

Being angry with the parents

And something else is also important. Such a child is angry with the real parents because they abandoned him or her. Deep inside the child is very upset with them. And this upset is often transferred to the adoptive parents. The child wants to protect the real parents, as it were, and the adoptive parents get the blows that are meant for the real ones.

To Viola: Was it like that with you? Then you can still make up for this, you can tell them that you take all of what they gave to you, as they gave it to you, and how great what they did for you is. That makes them glad, and they say to you: "It is alright, we gave it to you happily."

This is something we must consider. Therefore it does not help if we try to take the child to the real parents. And yet it is important for the child to have met the real parents. Where this is possible it would be good.

Example

There are situations in which one has to keep several things in mind. I will give you an example.

A minister wrote to me about a woman who became schizophrenic. She had a daughter who had to be placed into a foster family. The mother recovered and wanted her child back. The question was what he should advise the mother to do. My answer was, the daughter needs to stay with the foster parents, but the mother can say to her: "Now I am there for you again, and now you can come and see me any time. But I leave you with your foster parents who cared for you when I was ill." Then the child can go back and forth between the mother and the foster parents. But now the mother cannot take the child away from the foster parents any more. This would be considered an order of love, in which the child gets to have both her mother and the foster parents.

Youth services

PARTICIPANT: I am wondering about something that I see in my work. Sometimes the Department for Youth has to remove the children from families in a crisis situation. Very young children are put into foster families, mostly, to begin with, into an emergency care. But often it is the case that we do not succeed in activating the parents to the extent that they keep on being regular in relating to the child, once the child has been removed. Would the same apply here, too?

HELLINGER: Yes.

PARTICIPANT: This would mean, if one does not succeed with the parents, perhaps within a quarter of a year or over several months, one would definitely have to look for a foster family?

HELLINGER: Yes.

I once had such a case. I once had a course for mothers in an SOS children's village. One of these mothers was given away as a child. This mother had a child in her group who had been taken to the children's village, and now the mother wanted to take her child back. The question was, what would be a good solution here.

We did a constellation about this. I let the children's village mother represent this child. On the one side stood the children's

43

village mother, and on the other a representative for the biological mother, and the child stood in between.

There was a massive struggle in the soul of this child, hither and thither. For a long time the child was torn. Then the child stood next to the children's village mother. This was the right place.

PARTICIPANT: Concerning adoptions, you spoke about having no mercy for the parents, the parents who give the child away. I work in an adoption agency, and on the other hand, your statement was that adopted children cannot be happy when their biological parents do not receive a certain degree of respect. How do these two positions come together? Because, if I have no mercy, can I still have respect? Must I not have a bit of mercy, in order to bring some respect across?

HELLINGER: Where is the respect, in the toughness or in the mercy?

PARTICIPANT: In mercy.

HELLINGER: Where is the respect?

PARTICIPANT: In understanding the situation.

HELLINGER: If you have understanding and mercy, you turn them into children. I am hard, I make them grow up. Where is the respect in this?

PARTICIPANT: I don't know. Is this not contradictory?

HELLINGER: Many therapists behave like softies. They don't make people face the life they have, with all consequences. For instance: Every dog knows how to live and behave as a dog. We think that some people do not know how to live their lives as human beings, with all the consequences. Then they get soaked – through our mercy.

Love is strong, not weak.

Children in group homes

PARTICIPANT: This would also mean that children who have been in a group home for a long time do not have a realistic way back to their parents, because of the guilt?

HELLINGER: With a group home, I am not so sure. This is sometimes good because the child is relieved, and can return home again. With group homes it is a different situation than foster homes.

PARTICIPANT: Does the place make a difference?

HELLINGER: It depends on the whole situation. These days, many are of the opinion that a group home is something bad. I was in a boarding school for five years, and I felt released and relieved. Group homes can be proud about what they are doing.

Which adoptive parents?

PARTICIPANT: I have a question about the choice of adoptive parents. When we have a case where children suddenly become orphans, and the grandparents are willing to adopt the children, should they be considered with preference? Or should one look for the best adoptive parents for the children?

HELLINGER: One leaves the child in the family; this is the principle. Here the grandparents come first. Nobody can be better for a child than the grandparents, that cannot be.

So first of all, the grandparents, then the uncles and aunts. Only when there is no family member willing and able to take the child does one seek elsewhere. As far as possible, one leaves the child within the family, the clan.

PARTICIPANT: Even if these grandparents are perhaps also somewhat responsible for the death, let's say, of the mother?

HELLINGER: What do you mean, somewhat responsible?

PARTICIPANT: Well, if they have not supported their child enough to be fit for life, and if the child dies for this reason?

HELLINGER: These are interpretations of the worst kind. We must never assume such a thing. If the grandparents want to take their grandchild, this is the best place for the child. We must keep in mind that the child has a deep loyalty to the family and wants nothing more than to remain with the family. This even holds true for bad parents, even those who beat their children. The child wants to stay with them. If we take children away from their parents, assuming that they will be better off elsewhere, they punish themselves. We have to be very careful there, we must go with the child's soul. We must honor the child's loyalty and love. Where we do this, the child can grow. When we tear the child from the family because of outer considerations, it is bad.

It is particularly bad when a couple adopts a child from a country with a very different culture. It is better for the child to die in the homeland. There the child remains embedded in his fate. Many are of the opinion that they are entitled to intervene in the fate of a child, assuming the child will be happier then. But here we must be careful. There are exceptions, so I do not want to generalize here.

In choosing adoptive parents, it holds true that those who have children of their own are more suitable than those who have no children. But the youth departments know this anyhow, I don't need to tell them. For in the case where there are no other children, the adopted child is a replacement, and this is not good. Where adoptive parents are moved by their heart, where they want to help a child, then it is good. But where they cannot have a child of their own, and they act just because they don't have one, it is not good. But of course such parents may also be motivated by their wish to help a child, then that's different. This plays a big role.

Parents and adoptive parents

PARTICIPANT: Can you please say something about a helpful attitude of the adoptive parents towards the real parents?

HELLINGER: The adoptive parents must see themselves as the representatives of the biological parents. They must respect them. Only if they respect the parents can they respect the child. But if they feel superior to the biological parents, the child will take revenge and say: "You are not better than my parents."

Many years ago I did a course in transactional analysis. The group facilitator was a female pastor. She had adopted four children and also had several of her own. One of the children she adopted when he was already 6 or 7 years old. This child kept the whole family on their toes. He was, as one says, a psychopath, a terrible term. He was a poor child. After several years she said to the child: "You can do what you like, here I will remain your mother." Then the child broke down and said: "Mummy, for so many years I wanted you to become like my mother, now I give up." The child's mother was schizophrenic. This shows you the depth of the loyalty these children have.

All the best to you and say hello to your adoptive parents.

A foster child

HELLINGER *to a couple*: I will work with you now. I think you have a foster child. Come over here, then we stay with the topic.

What is the matter with the foster child?

WOMAN: The foster child went into a home when he was 9 years old, because the father had killed the mother. He went into a home with his siblings. He is the second oldest of four children.

HELLINGER: Do you also have children of your own?

WOMAN: I have two sons of my own, but we have no children together.

HELLINGER: What about the first husband?

WOMAN: He is married again and has another child.

HELLINGER: Did you get divorced?

WOMAN: Yes, but my two sons have different fathers.

HELLINGER: Were you married several times?

WOMAN: No, only once.

HELLINGER: It makes no difference. With a good product the circumstances don't matter. How old is the child now?

WOMAN: He is 19. He only came to us when he was 16.

HELLINGER: And how old was he when the father killed the mother?

WOMAN: He was 9.

HELLINGER: You took on quite a job.

WOMAN: I have the feeling it was imposed on us. The task was, to...

HELLINGER: The child will become a murderer. The child will become a murderer unless we find a solution.

I had a supervision group in Kassel. There was a woman who said that her sister's husband had killed her sister, and the two children came to her. I am just saying this in preparation for what we have here.

Then I did a constellation. The representative of the woman's sister moved away from the husband immediately, full of fear. The husband just stood there and looked to the floor. Then I laid her on the floor, for she was dead after all, and I got the man to look in that direction.

When a murderer is in a constellation, the person doesn't know where to look, and his or her breath is very shallow. So I took this man to the dead woman, and I got him to look at her and to breathe deeply. Suddenly the pain came up in him. An incredible pain. He went down to the woman, and they embraced. Murderers and victims are often connected in a deep love.

There they were, lying together, and the children and their aunt stood further away. One child -- they were two girls -- wanted to go to the father, the other wanted to go to the mother. Then I got them to lie there, and I said: One girl will become a murderer, the other a victim. This is how loyalty works.

Then I intervened, I asked the girls to get up, and the father said to the children: Go to your aunt. The mother also said: Go to your aunt. Then the aunt took them into her arms. Then they turned away, and the two girls felt relieved, quite relieved, and they could go on.

These are the dynamics in such a case. What is going on in this family here, we must see. We need a representative for the boy, a representative for the father and a representative for his mother.

The representatives for the father and the mother stand next to each other. The representative for the son stands opposite them. After a while he slowly raises his hands as if he wants to go for someone's throat.

HELLINGER: This is the perpetrator energy. One can see that he will become a murderer.
To the woman: How did he kill her?
WOMAN: He cut her throat.
HELLINGER: And what happened to him?
WOMAN: He is in a psychiatric ward.

The father clenches his fists and holds them up in front of his face. The mother is shaking. The son wants to go to the father, but Hellinger stops him.

After a while Hellinger asks the mother to lie on the floor. The father also goes down to the floor. After a while they embrace. Hellinger asks the son to go to them and to put his arms around both of them. Mother and father are sobbing. The son strokes the mother. After a while Hellinger takes the son away from them. The son gets up, and Hellinger turns him away from the parents.

Then he chooses a man and places the son in front of him.
HELLINGER: I take you, you are fate.
To the son: Bow to this.
After a while: Look back once more and look at your parents. And this is the image you take into your heart. Now turn around again.

Hellinger asks the fate to stand behind the son.

HELLINGER *to the son*: How are you now?
SON: Good. Here I find peace.
HELLINGER: Now I leave it here. Thank you to the representatives.
To the foster parents: Do you have an image now?
WOMAN: Yes, thank you.
HELLINGER: But you must not say anything to him. Entrust him to his parents as you saw this here. Now you can look at them with love and respect. This is a heavy fate for all involved, but how much love there is with them in the end! There he is safe. You need not separate him from his parents. Okay? Good.

HELLINGER *to the group*: Of course, then I think in what kind of fatal entanglement this boy's father was. What happened in his family? The way the son is, or was, at risk of becoming a murderer, perhaps the father ended up in this situation through some entanglement. So he was not free. You can see how the distinction between good and bad is harder and harder to make.

I think we can leave it here for today. It was a rich day, this must sink in now. It is good if you don't talk about it, and you simply let it find its place in your soul. Okay? Good.

A further comment

HELLINGER: I want to say something else about these constellations. They work through the image. Every explanation we attempt to give injures the image. Talking about it robs the image of its strength. The image is an image of the soul, from the depth of the soul. If we enter this sphere with our intellect, with a range of interpretations, the soul withdraws.

Now we can let everything pass before our inner eye once more, all the things that came to light today. What depth of soul! In what entanglements the individuals are caught! How big each individual family is in its particularity, with everything that happened there! If we grasp that, we become humble. Coming from this humility we can also deal much better with heavy fates, and also with those who have such a heavy fate. At ease, we trust in greater powers.

To conclude the day, I will tell you a little story. I don't know why I choose this one, but it will be good for something. The story is called, "The Path."

The path

A son found his way back to his old father and he begged him: Father, bless me before you go. The father said: My blessing shall be that I will walk with you on the path of knowledge for a little while. The next morning they stepped out into the open, and from the narrow valley they climbed a mountain.

The day was already bent down by the time they reached the summit, but now the land was bathed in light in all directions, as far as the eye could see.

The sun began to sink, and with it, all the glorious splendor, and then night fell. But as darkness surrounded them, the stars were shining.

Consequences of a rape

HELLINGER *to a woman*: Now it's your turn. What is it about?

WOMAN: I was adopted, born in 1947. I was with my mother for four weeks, and half a year later I was given up for adoption. Three years ago I found my biological mother. I have a half brother and a half sister.

Through my documents I found out that I am the child of a rape. In my documents it says that my mother was raped by two Polish soldiers in April 1946. Nobody ever talked to me about my father. And I did not think about him either. It could have easily been like this for my whole life.

HELLINGER: This is enough. Someone said to me in a course: "I am the child of a rape." I said to him: "For you it is a blessing."

WOMAN: Yes.

HELLINGER *to the group*: We must see it this way. I once led a constellation in Holland. Then one man said: "My grandmother was raped by nine Russians." Then I set these nine Russians up and also added the grandfather. The grandfather did not look at his wife at all. His gaze went into the distance, probably to his dead comrades. His wife stood next to the rapists and said: "At least they look at me."

I will do a simple constellation. I need two soldiers, and someone who represents her and someone for her mother.

Hellinger places the woman's mother opposite the two soldiers, and her daughter a little bit further away.

52

The mother stands there with clenched fists. One of the soldiers reaches his hand out to her. The mother slowly goes towards him and takes his outstretched hand. The daughter goes to stand next to the mother.

The soldier puts his right hand around her. Then they embrace, and she puts her head on his shoulder. Then she strokes his face, and they embrace tenderly. The daughter withdraws, and the second soldier also. The mother stands behind this other soldier, and he embraces her from behind. The first soldier gets on his knees and cries loudly.

HELLINGER *to the woman*: How are you?

WOMAN: Good.

HELLINGER: Where does your gaze go?

WOMAN: To the father.

HELLINGER: Who is it?

The woman points to the soldier who cries on the floor.

WOMAN: Him.

HELLINGER: Okay, I leave it here.

To the group: Strange things come to light here.

To the woman: How are you?

WOMAN: I am fine.

HELLINGER *to the group:* Who could ever unveil the secrets of love? One thing is very important to know. The mother who rejects the man, also rejects the child.

To the woman: Therefore she gave you away. And how do you become whole? By taking your father into your heart. You are a part of him. Is it okay like that? Can we leave it like that? Okay. Good.

A disabled child

HELLINGER *to the group*: I'll continue working.

To the mother of a disabled child: What about your child, what is the child's disability?

MOTHER: Medically, it is an inherited illness of the metabolism, with a low life-expectancy and no chances of healing.

HELLINGER: How old is the child now?

MOTHER: 10½.

HELLINGER: Is it a boy or a girl?

MOTHER: It is a boy, Martin.

HELLINGER: What about his father?

MOTHER: We separated seven years ago, but in caring for the child we take turns, weekend for weekend. He is fully behind him. He is totally behind him and also behind me. All these years he was by our side.

HELLINGER: What troubles you now?

MOTHER: I had periods of a bad conscience again and again, for having given him up. This feeling comes back to me all the time. I know he is well cared for, but I can't get over it.

HELLINGER: I think in one of my books I have a story about a mother with a disabled child who is in a home. This was very moving for me.

Now we will have a look at this, and I take you into the constellation right now. Just stand there.

Hellinger chooses a representative for the disabled boy and asks him to stand opposite the mother.

The disabled boy stands opposite his mother. After a while Hellinger chooses a representative for the boy's father and also places him. The father looks at the boy, and the mother withdraws. Then the father takes a few steps closer to the son, reaches out with his right hand and strokes the boy's cheek. He withdraws his hand again, and he slowly goes to the floor. He stretches his arms out and looks to the floor. The boy also goes to the floor, kneels beside his father and does the same movements. The mother cries. Then the father reaches out to the boy's head and strokes it for a long time. As he does this, he continues to look at the floor.

HELLINGER *to the mother*: Do you know what this means?

MOTHER: I have nothing to do with this.

HELLINGER: What happened in your husband's family?

MOTHER: Martin's grandfather had a brother whom he lost very early. That's all I know.

HELLINGER: There is something mighty going on.

She shakes her head.

HELLINGER: Where does the illness come from? Is it an inherited illness?

WOMAN: It is an inherited illness from both sides. It is a genetic defect.

HELLINGER: From your side and from his side?

MOTHER: Yes, from both sides.

Hellinger asks her to kneel in front of the two. The father draws the boy still closer to him. Without getting up from the floor with the son, he stretches one hand out to the mother who takes his hand. The father draws the son still closer to him. The son looks at the father. Then the mother also strokes the son's head, but then she withdraws her hand again.

The father gets up on his knees. Both parents stroke the boy's back with one hand, while holding each other by the other hand.

After a while the husband strokes his wife's face with one hand, and she puts her head on the son.

55

HELLINGER: I think I can leave it here.

to the mother: A love that is taken to task by reality in such a way, what greatness and what power does it have in the end. Such depth is not reached by ordinary love.

The two of you must of course come back together. Guilt feelings are in the way. However, you walk with your life's path, and then all is well. Alright like this?

Okay, all the best to you.

Story: Freedom

HELLINGER *to the group*: I will tell you a little story:

A student asked a master: Tell me what freedom is.

Which freedom? asked the master.

The first freedom is foolishness. It is like a horse that throws off his rider, neighing, yet all the tighter will it feel its rider's grip from hereon.

The second freedom is regret. It is like the helmsman who remains on board after the shipwreck, instead of getting into a lifeboat.

The third freedom is insight. Unfortunately, it comes after foolishness and regret. It is like the reed that sways in the wind and gives in when it is weak, and therefore it still stands.

The student asked: Is this all?

The master replied: Some think that they are the ones who seek the truth of their souls. But the great soul thinks and seeks through them. Just like nature, the great soul can afford a huge amount of errors, for false players can be replaced at any time and effortlessly. But to those who let the great soul think through them, it grants them sometimes a little room to move. And like a swimmer who lets himself drift, the soul carries him in a joint effort, to new shores.

Supervision

HELLINGER: Now we will look at supervision cases. Who wants to present a supervision case?

A boy who was burned

HELLINGER: *to a caretaker*: What is this case about?

CARETAKER: I have been looking after a boy for ten years. He suffered very severe burns at the age of 3. It is a miracle that he survived. His mother died in the fire. He only met his father three years ago, but there is no contact.

HELLINGER: Why could the boy not know his father?

CARETAKER: The parents were separated. The mother had thrown the father out. At first the boy grew up with the grandparents. He also experienced a lot of outer injuries. This means, he was quite rejected because of his monster-like appearance.

HELLINGER: How did the fire originate?

CARETAKER: He probably caused it.

HELLINGER: The boy?

CARETAKER: Yes. He lived in a communal household, where nobody looked after him. The mother was drug addicted, and there is the assumption that he played with fire.

HELLINGER: Who caused the fire?

CARETAKER: Certainly not him.

HELLINGER: It was the mother, obviously. From the circumstances, we can never blame the child. How old is he now?

CARETAKER: 18.

HELLINGER: What else is a problem?

CARETAKER: He has been living with us for ten years. He chose the home himself. He wanted to come. Until now he did everything: school and a trade. But he has no joy of living. He tends to be depressed. Every now and then I have the feeling that he is suffocated by all these unresolved matters.

HELLINGER: Why did the father not show an interest all these years?

CARETAKER: We don't know.

HELLINGER: Was there any attempt to contact him?

CARETAKER: The grandparents did, but they controlled it a bit, to protect the boy.

HELLINGER: He must be with his father. From the beginning he should have been with his father, with no one else. Okay, this would be one case.

HELLINGER *after a long interlude*: Now I will continue with the case of the burned boy. We will set up the child, the mother, the father, the grandparents. I will choose, and then you set them up.

The mother stands in front of the boy. Her parents stand behind her. The father stands alone.

The boy puts one hand in front of his belly, then both hands in front of his mouth and his throat. The mother has both hands in front of her chest. Her mother and her father stand there with clenched fists, especially the father. After a while Hellinger turns the woman to face her parents. The boy's father had moved towards the boy in the meantime. Father and son embrace tenderly.

HELLINGER I think this will do. There is a murderous energy, taken on by the mother's father. Something must have happened there. Look at his fists. The boy must go to his father. He could not go to his mother, because it was too murderous there.

HELLINGER *to the boy's maternal grandfather*: What is happening with you?

BOY'S MATERNAL GRANDFATHER: An incredible rage. It is incomprehensible. And icy cold shivers.

HELLINGER: Something happened there. That's where it is. Okay? Good, thank you all.

To the representative of the boy's maternal grandfather: Get out of this. Best of all, you bow briefly before the one you represented, and then you turn away. Good? Okay.

HELLINGER *after a while to the caretaker*: Do you know what you can say to the boy? Better burned than a murderer.

The dream father

HELLINGER *to two caretakers*: What is your issue?

FIRST CARETAKER: In our institution we had a caretaker relationship for over ten years, with four siblings in a row. They developed very differently and in very difficult ways, which made it difficult in the foster family. Our assessment was that the foster parents had not internalized the respect for the system of origin, that it was rather a verbal commitment.

Additionally, there were themes from the system of origin. There were many, many dead people. As I said before, there are four children, two of them are boys. The two boys go in a direction where they have already tried to take their own lives, they put themselves into dangerous situations and also along criminal paths. The girls took somewhat different paths, which were not very healthy either.

HELLINGER: So there are two boys and two girls?

FIRST CARETAKER: Yes.

HELLINGER: And what do you know about the family of origin?

FIRST CARETAKER: The biological mother has six children altogether, from three different men. The first two, a boy and a girl, from one man. All three men have been behind bars. Alcohol and violence featured in this. The most obvious in the system is in the family of the father of those two oldest children. There were thirteen children in his system of origin. Ten of these thirteen children died young. They died during the war, fleeing their homeland, from starvation or accidents.

HELLINGER: I would like to look at this together with you. I will do it separately, taking the children from one father at a time, because there are different fates. So let us take what you said last, the family in which ten children died.

Why was the father imprisoned?

FIRST CARETAKER: Officially because he was behind paying maintenance for the children.

HELLINGER: Officially only, for sure. What was the real reason?

FIRST CARETAKER: There's dead silence about that. We only know the superficial level.

HELLINGER: For how long was he in prison?

FIRST CARETAKER: For about two years.

HELLINGER: Does it exist at all, imprisonment because of failure to pay maintenance? Does this exist? And for so long? I am not familiar with such matters, I have to ask.

FIRST CARETAKER: There is another story too about this. The mother was seven months pregnant with the second child. The man wanted her to come back to him. They had separated. He stood in front of the flat with a pistol and told her she had to come back to him. He went to the mother, threatened her and said: I want you to come back to me. In that moment, labor set in, and the child was born prematurely, at seven months, weighing just 100 grams. To survive this was still very difficult 20 years ago, but the boy survived.

HELLINGER: The older girl is his sister?

FIRST CARETAKER: The older girl is the sister. There is about one year between the children.

HELLINGER: What about the father's father?

FIRST CARETAKER: With the father's father there were also the themes of alcohol and violence. There was tension in the family, but more is not known.

HELLINGER: So this is the family in which ten children died?

FIRST CARETAKER: Yes, this is the father.

HELLINGER: Are these two the oldest children of the mother?

FIRST CARETAKER: Yes, they are the oldest children of the mother and also of the father. They were both very young, 19 and 20 years old.

HELLINGER: I will begin with the father and the mother.

To the caretaker: Choose and set them up.

The first caretaker chooses a father and mother and places them opposite each other. There is no movement between them.

Hellinger chooses a woman for the oldest child from this relationship and places her with the parents. After a while the father goes towards the mother and reaches out his hand to her. After some hesitation she goes to him and puts her head on his chest. Both of them look at the girl.

HELLINGER: *after a while to this girl*: What is with you?

GIRL: I can hardly bear it to see them like that. I feel rage inside. I don't trust his smile. I want to say to him: Don't lie to me. I am really dizzy in the head.

HELLINGER *to the caretaker*: Did the two have earlier relationships?

FIRST CARETAKER: Well, the mother was abused by her father.

The parents look at each other and smile.

HELLINGER: Seen from the whole movement, the problem is not with the father. It is clearly with the mother.

Hellinger chooses a representative for the mother's father and places him opposite her at some distance. The first man holds the mother all the more tightly.

Hellinger gets the man to stand farther away, so that the woman is opposite her father. The mother begins to sway. Hellinger put his hand on her back. She covers her face with her hands and begins to sob.

HELLINGER *to the mother*: Look at him.

She goes slowly towards her father and then puts her arms around his neck. They embrace each other tightly for a long time.

HELLINGER *after a while to the girl*: How is it?
GIRL: I can gladly look at this.

After a while, the mother and her father look at each other. The mother wants to move away from her father.

HELLINGER: Go with the movement.
After a while: The movement goes in another direction. Lower your head.
Again, after some moments: Okay, and now withdraw.

She slowly goes back. Hellinger places her daughter by her side, and the two put their arms around each other sideways.

Hellinger points to the daughter's father.

HELLINGER *to the mother*: Tell her: This is your father.

MOTHER: This is your father.

HELLINGER: In the mother's image, her own father was also her child's father, and it was the same image for the daughter.

Hellinger chooses a representative for the mother's mother and places her at some distance from her husband. The girl stands in front of her. She does not look at the grandfather.

HELLINGER: She does not look at her husband at all.

Now the girl's father goes slowly towards her. Both embrace tenderly.

HELLINGER: Strange relationships, when we look at all of this.

After a while: I will interrupt it here. Everything is upside down here. I thank you.

To the two caretakers: You have a difficult task here.

SECOND CARETAKER: As an institution we have not been able to do anything other than collect information. Even in the case conferences the foster parents never opened up to really having a look at the situation. It was impossible.

HELLINGER: The children aren't in good hands there. But at least you can understand the girl better, and what her entanglement is.

FATHER: Well, nothing separated me from my daughter any more. There was something frightening coming from the mother's side. That was strong.

HELLINGER: Now we must let it rest, and then perhaps, through the goodwill to understand, something that will help you to find another approach will show up in the soul.

Perpetrators and victims

CARETAKER: Can you say something general about dealing with perpetrators and victims? According to what is suggested here again and again, good and bad is apparently not what it seems. Can you say a bit more about it in this connection?

HELLINGER: With good and bad it is usually the opposite of what is presented. Here in this family we could see: The negative force was with the mother, with the mother's mother.

CARETAKER: My question is about, well, we have to deal with perpetrators again and again, or we have to relate to them anyhow. The perpetrators are rejected again and again, the abusers are rejected. This seems to be completely wrong. There must be other ways, for with this approach we don't get anywhere.

HELLINGER: We can only relate to a perpetrator if we give him a place in our heart. Then he softens, not before. Every attack hardens him more. We have to be very careful about this. I give you an example:

Many years ago I had a course in Switzerland. A social worker told me about a girl who was abused by her grandfather and by her uncle. The social worker wanted to tell the police. I warned him not to do it. It is bad for the child if the perpetrators are denounced.

A few years later I met him again, and he told me that the two had been sentenced. Then I asked him how the girl was. He said she keeps on wanting to jump out of the window.

This is what the denouncing achieved. The victims are loyal, even though it is forbidden to show this. We saw it here, the general pressure says that it is something terrible – so they are not allowed to show the love.

The worst isn't really the act. I don't want to brush over it, but the level of emotion that certain circles of people put into their reaction discourages the child from showing real feelings. And it is quite clear: There is very deep love. Only when this is acknowledged can we do the other things that release the child from this entanglement. In this regard this is a very important step.

I'll give you an example. In Mexico we had a constellation with a female holocaust survivor. She was fairly aggressive. Then I placed representatives for the victims and the perpetrators. And she stood in front of the perpetrators, challenging them. One of them said to her: "For as long as you look at me like this, I get stronger and stronger, when you become humble, I can't hold myself up any longer."

Most perpetrators feel superior. When a social worker feels superior to a perpetrator he or she becomes a perpetrator, just like the perpetrator. The feeling of superiority has the effect that we become like the perpetrator. We also have aggressive feelings, and we drag the perpetrator before the court. Then we are exactly like the perpetrator, fighting him in this way. We have to be very careful in this. In such matters I always keep an eye on the child. I ask myself what goes on in the soul of the child. Of course this doesn't mean that I am in favor of not dealing with these matters before the court. But these are two different matters. One thing is a matter of the government. But one who has a responsibility for the child must not be mixed up by these domains. A caretaker cannot go into this prosecution mode at the same time that he or she is trying to care for the child. Only in this way can we help.

CARETAKER: I have a question about the persons who stood there as representatives now. When in a case of abuse a woman is chosen as the representative of the abused person, and she had been abused herself, does she respond differently than a woman who has not experienced abuse? Does this make a difference to the constellation?

HELLINGER: Generally not. If it was the case, she can, through the experience, also solve something for herself.

Abortions

HELLINGER: Who had another supervision case? What was it with you?

CARETAKER: I have been looking after a family for the last half year, a very young family with three little children. Both parents grew up in group homes. Their oldest child was in a foster family for a short time, and in this family there is enormous tension, a massive pressure, so that the children behave as if they are trained animals. Even the dog gets out of the way when the father comes home.

HELLINGER: Was one of the parents in another relationship before?

CARETAKER: No, they got together very young, but there are also a lot of stories of children who were given away, and he does not know...

HELLINGER: No, no, no. I remain with the question: Was there an earlier relationship?

CARETAKER: No, there is no knowledge about that.

HELLINGER: It is quite clear that the man has to represent someone from the woman's family.

CARETAKER: Perhaps her brother, he is in jail. The mother was married five times and then she had two more partners. The children from the first two marriages were taken from her and adopted out. The mother's mother had two children, one of them is the mother, and she has a brother who is in jail now because of drugs. Then there is also another child from a later ...

HELLINGER *to the group*: Whom did she not mention?

CARETAKER: The father of the two.

HELLINGER: Exactly, and he's the important one. Everything that is not mentioned is important.

This is enough for me. Now we begin with a constellation: the father, the mother, the three children, and a dog, for the dog is also a representative, of course.

The woman's representative presses her hands tightly against her ears. The youngest child falls down and lies on the floor.

Hellinger chooses a representative for the woman's father and places him in front of her. She still covers her ears with her hands, then turns away and takes a few steps away from the center.

Hellinger chooses a representative for the woman's mother and places her next to the woman's father.

HELLINGER *to the woman*: Turn around. Open your eyes.

She keeps on pressing both her hands tightly to her head.

HELLINGER *to the caretakers*: Seen from the reaction, something very terrible must have happened.

HELLINGER *to the woman*: What do you see?
WOMAN: My head. Beating. Head squashed.

Hellinger chooses a further female representative and gets her to lie down on her back between the woman and her mother and her father. The woman is still holding her head with both hands. Then she moves backwards. Her mother goes towards her. The woman flees from her, and her mother runs after her. When the woman passes her husband, he takes her in his arms and holds her tight.

HELLINGER *to the woman's mother*: Look at the floor, look at the floor, at the dead woman who is lying there.

The woman's mother turns around to the dead woman. Then she gets down on her knees and touches her. After a while the woman takes her hands off her head. She leans into her husband. The two hold each other.

HELLINGER *after a while to the first child*: What is with you?

FIRST CHILD: I want to leave, I want to get out of here, I don't want to look there. I sway between drooping down and trying to muster my strength. I want to get away.

HELLINGER *to the caretaker*: There was a murder in the family. We also saw it in the reaction of the third child who fell to the floor. The question is just, where.

CARETAKER: I only know about an abortion that happened before her. I am not aware of anything else.

HELLINGER: I stop it here. I leave it there as it is. Thanks to the representatives.

HELLINGER: How was it for the dog?

DOG: I felt for my master.

HELLINGER *to the group*: So, about the way of proceeding here. I stopped twice, without trying to investigate further. This is the right procedure. As soon as something does not move further, one stops. Stopping is a therapeutic measure. We acknowledge the boundaries that are set for us. Usually it is at the height of the energy where one stops. Then something gets moving in the soul. Not in our own soul, but in the system's soul, something begins to move. We must trust in that. We received an important piece of information about the head. There was something with a head. I would take that seriously. Then one waits and sees. Something is set into motion. This is enough for the beginning.

To the caretakers: I admire more and more what you take on.

CARETAKER WHO PRESENTED THE CASE: I still have a short question. The father is very aggressive, verbally aggressive. Can this have something to do with this, or does this rather have something to do with his family of origin? Because he notices that he breaks off with anyone and anything and is afraid he might kill someone and will have to be constantly on the run from authorities.

HELLINGER: This is of course also something special about his situation. But here he was the calmer one. And he has to keep in mind the strange phenomenon in partner relationships that one of them might take on the burden of the other. This goes all the way to the extreme that one partner commits suicide in the place of the other. We have to be careful there. But it was clear to me, we had to begin with the mother. Usually it is the other way round. You wanted to begin with the father, but here it is the other way round.

CARETAKER: I have another question concerning the constellation. How do I deal with it, that the family will want to know what the constellation revealed? They did not come along, but the question will come up of course. How can one handle that?

HELLINGER: Tell them exactly what went on, without commenting; one child fell down, one turned away, one held his head, exactly that. Only tell them what was, and no further questions. Then wait to see what will come of it.

CARETAKER: Without any evaluation either?

HELLINGER: Without evaluation, this is very important, only to say what went on.

Abortions (continued)

CARETAKER: I have the question about what consequences abortions have, also because I work in pregnancy-conflict

69

counseling. Or does timing make a difference? I have heard the question: When did the abortion take place?

HELLINGER: If it is a late abortion, it is experienced like murder. If it was an early termination, then not always as murder. It is sometimes experienced differently. But there are some strange connections.

I had a course in Russia, in Moscow. There was a couple who said they could not have children, and they would like to have children, and they asked if I could help them.

I looked at the woman and she was quite cheerful. I told her that she obviously didn't want children. I asked her what happened in her family of origin. Then she became quite serious. Her mother had had eight abortions. Then I got eight representatives for the aborted children to sit on the floor, and she sat next to them. She felt good there. Then I got them all to stand again, with all the aborted children behind her. I placed her husband by her side, and in front of them a representative for their future child.

It was quite clear, she receives the strength and the courage to have children of her own from the aborted siblings. So these aborted children belong to the family.

Another example. In a course in Verona there was a woman who said she was afraid her children might die. I placed her, her husband and the two children, and in front of them death, a man. He went down to the floor immediately and sat there. This is not what death does. It was clear that this man represented a child. Then I asked the woman about what happened in her mother's family. She said her mother had had nine abortions, and she was bragging about that.

We set up the nine aborted children and their mother behind them. Immediately the mother began to cry violently and she sat down next to her aborted children. It was clear, the death that the woman feared, was her mother. From there we could find a solution for her.

Abortions leave a deep trace in the soul, a very deep trace. This is often denied, with all kinds of plausible reasoning. The soul does not listen to these reasons. We say sometimes that abortion is like a kind of contraception, in Japan for instance. Still, it is experienced the same way there as it is with us here. There is no difference. It is experienced as a deep interference in the soul.

The aborted children belong to the family and they are experienced that way. If this comes to light and the children are included in the family, it has a beneficial effect.

Forgiving or persecuting

CARETAKER: I have a short question about the difference between forgiving and judicial prosecution. At work I have a woman who was cheated out of all money after her divorce. She can't find peace, because she is constantly tormenting herself with the question: Shall I take him to court, or shall I let go of it? She does not find peace with this question. I don't know what I shall advise her to do.

HELLINGER: You must advise her to say: "I knew what kind of a rogue you are, and now I accept the consequences." Then she can find peace.

CARETAKER: But she insists she did not know.

HELLINGER: Shall we set it up? Okay.

Hellinger chooses representatives for the woman, the man, and the money.

The representative for the money stands big and strong, in front of the man, with his hands on his hips, and he looks to the man. The woman withdraws quite a long way. The money looks at the man, posturing triumphantly. The man sways. The woman turns away and wants to leave. The man and the money stand opposite each other, while the money is still triumphant.

HELLINGER *to the caretaker*: Okay, now you only need to imagine: What would happen if the woman received the money?

Hellinger calls the representative for the woman back and places the money opposite her. She is shocked and holds her hands in front of her chest to ward something off.

HELLINGER: *to the caretaker*: But there is something else that is important. I would ask her: Who in your family has lost a lot of money? She is secretly loyal to this person.

A boy at risk

HELLINGER: Is there anything you wish to add to what happened this morning? Okay, who else had supervision cases? You?

Okay, what is it about?

CARETAKER: I have been working in a family-like household group. This means I am in charge of this group and care for four children. In this supervision it is largely about the boy who is now the oldest, 16 years old, who is becoming increasingly aggressive. I notice that it gets more and more difficult in the group.

HELLINGER: How old is he?

CARETAKER: 16 years.

HELLINGER: What about his parents?

CARETAKER: He has no contact with his parents. In eleven years he saw his mother once, at his request. He phoned her a few times, and then it petered out again.

HELLINGER: How old was he when he came into this home and into this group?

CARETAKER: The children were taken, so he is with us in this group with two siblings. Three other siblings were in another group.

HELLINGER: Why were they taken?

CARETAKER: The father committed crimes, thefts, several criminal actions. Then one night the children were taken from their parents, by the police, with the siren going.

HELLINGER: What about the mother?

CARETAKER: The mother was also in prison for a short time.

HELLINGER: What for?

CARETAKER: It looked as if she was an accessory to the act. There was also violence in the family, physical violence.

HELLINGER: What does this mean? What happened?

CARETAKER: Sascha was definitely beaten. Cigarettes were extinguished on his back. He was the punching bag, and once he was up for sale via an illegal institute.

HELLINGER: We set it up: The father, the mother, and the son.

Hellinger places the father opposite the son, at some distance. But the father looks to the side. The mother stands somewhat away from the family. After a while Hellinger guides the father away from the family, farther in the direction that he looked.

HELLINGER *to the father*: Is this better or worse?

FATHER: Better.

HELLINGER *to the son*: And for you?

SON: A bit better, when he goes. I must brace myself. I ask myself, what do they want from me? I have a hostile attitude. I don't know what's going on here.

HELLINGER *to the caretaker*: Do you know what happened in the father's family?

CARETAKER: What is going on in the family I don't know. But all in all it is a very chaotic situation in the family.

HELLINGER: What happens there? Earlier on I had the impulse to ask you to stand where you feel it is your place. Where would you have stood? Do it from your feeling.

The caretaker stands to the right of the son.

HELLINGER *to the father*: Go back to your place once more.
HELLINGER *after a while to the son*: How is it when she stands there?
SON: It is strange, as if the air is drawn out if me. At first it weakens me, even though in some way it also feels good.

Hellinger places the caregiver next to the father, on his right side.

HELLINGER *to the son*: How is this for you?
SON: This is good.
HELLINGER *to the father*: And for you?
FATHER: Before I had the sentence: "I am not aware of any wrongdoing." But when she stands there, I can't get out.
HELLINGER *to the group*: I just demonstrated something about systemic connections. The helper is successful if he or she stands next to the most rejected and despised person. This has the greatest effect. We could see this here. I think I can leave it there.
If you get it across to the boy that he can respect his father, he will feel better. We could see that he is suicidal. He has to get away, the direction points that way. There must be something quite heavy in his family. When I consider all of this, I can understand and respect him. The boy is different immediately. Okay, that's it then.

It is always the family member who is not mentioned, who is shunned and demonized, who needs to have a place in the system. As soon as the excluded person gets a place, the system as a whole is already healed, because the system is whole again. Then everyone else can find a new orientation again.

CARETAKER: So the fact that he went away and feels good about it cannot mean that the man is not his father?

HELLINGER: Seen from the boy's reaction, the man is his father, otherwise he would not be so involved. Usually wanting-to-get-away means at least suicidal, that he wants to disappear, for whatever reasons.

This movement sets in when someone is in an absolutely frightful situation, in which there are no options left. In his soul he is the most miserable of all.

CARETAKER: Would it be a good idea, or would it be too much, if one would support contact with the father?

HELLINGER: You only say to the boy: "I respect your father. When I look at you, I think, you do have a proper father." Something like that, just a little comment. But you won't even have to say that. When you get back, you will be changed anyhow.

Measured action

CARETAKER: I don't have a direct question, but perhaps you could say something about this. In our role as caretakers we have seen here what consequences our actions have according to the extent of the influence we exert or don't exert. There's also this feeling in me again and again, and the challenge to be a kind of judge even though I don't want that. Nevertheless there is a task, an inner task that I also have.

HELLINGER: Today someone gave me a book: *A Little Soul Is Talking to God*. It says something to God, that it would so love to be forgiveness. Then God asks: "Who is it then whom you want to forgive?"

The little soul looked around and could not find anything. God said: "In my creation there is nothing to forgive – and even less, to judge."

The worst is if we have pity for the children. Pity weakens them incredibly. You look at their fate, and you respect their fate. You don't know what will come of it in the end. If you intervene, you perhaps intervene in a way that is in opposition to this fate. If you are just there with respect, before the parents, before the greater whole, then after some time perhaps something good can develop. Then you have your peace. Many who want to help exhaust themselves in trying. When you go into an attitude of respect, you can't exhaust yourself so easily. But of course it does happen. There are situations where we have to exhaust ourselves, but it should not be ongoing stress.

I sometimes have an attitude when I work or when a client looks at me. Then I let the person look through me. The gaze does not come to me. The person looks through me, to something greater. Then when I work with this person, I let what is behind me, something greater, flow through me – towards this person. At other times I might step aside, so that they can come into immediate contact with each other. This helps to bring ease. Then we can see what happens to the children with whom we have a task, when we bring this ease along with us. The beautiful image is: We let the sun shine, and sometimes there is lightning, and then there's rain, just as it comes and goes.

Applied group dynamics

HELLINGER: In South Africa I was in charge of a home, a boarding school with 140 boys. We only had one prefect for them. They did everything in self-management. It can be done.

Someone told me about another boarding school in South Africa, where all caretakers got ill. The students had to organize everything themselves. It never worked as well again as in that time.

Something like that I can also tell you about myself. I became the principal of a large elite school in South Africa, and at the same time I was the priest of a large parish. During the Easter holidays, and the Maundy days, some boys could go home. The others stayed on.

They asked me if they could go to Durban for half of the day, for entertainment. I said yes, but said they'd have to be back for the service in the afternoon. As a priest I needed some of them to read to the parishioners and as ministrants. But they returned at 8 pm; those responsible had encouraged them to stay longer. I, as the priest, then had to do everything myself on Maundy Thursday. I had only been the principal of this school for a short time. So they had tested me.

Now I tell you something about applied group dynamics. The laws of group dynamics with which I had been familiar, and which I could apply in this school, had to prove themselves. As a result, each class had someone responsible whom they had chosen, and from the higher grades, five students were chosen from the whole school. Together they got the whole organization going.

This evening, my co-brother and I called those who were responsible into my office. There we sat, and neither we nor them spoke a single word. A quarter of an hour passed, and not a word was uttered. They did not know what to do. This was a method of group dynamics.

Then I said: "The discipline of the school has broken down, and we can't act any more. The question is, whether my co-brother and I still want to do anything, for you must win us over again, if you want us to do something for you again. We will give you a chance to restore discipline."

The next day they called all the students together, and they discussed the matter, about how the discipline of the school could be restored. Then they made us an offer. But it was worthless. I said: "That's not good enough." Then they talked about it for another four hours. After that they made another offer: "We will give up a whole day during the holidays to restore the sports floors to order." I said: "I agree." Then one of the students said: "All of this only happened because two of you were not back in time for the service." I immediately dismissed him from the school. But four weeks later he was allowed to enroll again.

They began to tidy up the sports floors. After half a day I said: "It's good enough."

I never had discipline problems again at this school.

The other love

HELLINGER: Now we leave the level of supervision and we go to the level of couple relationships. Then all wake up again immediately. I would be willing to work with something like that now, so that you can go home with something lighter on your mind.

First of all I would like to say something about "the other love". When the man meets the woman, and the woman the man, they look into each other's eyes, and suddenly they are fascinated. Then there is love at first sight. How much strength does this love at first sight have?

When we measure it on a scale of 0 to 100 according to energy and strength, where would we place the love at first sight? My image is, ten percent. For the love at first sight is a love without sight. We do not see the other yet, but only a dreamy image. I will not elucidate this further. Usually we see the perfect mother. Both men and women see the ideal mother, but this is not so important.

When the man says to the woman: "I love you," and the woman says: "I love you," there is little power. This love cannot last long.

But we can say something different that would be the other love then. The man can say to the woman, and the woman can say to the man: "I love you, and I love that which guides me and you."Suddenly the gaze is widened towards something greater, at whose mercy both of them are, in a special way. What this means shows itself in the course of time.

It may be that this other love guides the couple on the same path for a time. Especially if they have children, this other love guides them on a certain path for a long time. After some time it can happen that something else moves into the foreground, for instance, if a child is disabled. Suddenly something else takes center stage, something far more powerful, which they could never encounter with their love at first sight. Then they can say to each other, for instance: "I love you and that which guides you and me." They look at the child and tell the child: "I love you and that which guides you and me." Both partners say it, and suddenly a completely different sphere becomes visible. It can also happen that after some time it becomes clear that both of them are led in a way that they move away from their partner, and have to do so, if they wish to remain in accord with something greater. This becomes unavoidable for both of them.

Then they tell each other: "I love you and that which guides me and you." Even if their paths separate, this love remains.

This is the other love. I also call it: Love at second sight. Then reality comes into play in its fullness.

We can also apply that to children, and to such heavy cases from your work as you showed us today. "I love you and that which guides you and me."

Sometimes I notice I am not guided by anything that could help anyone. The person is guided by something, but I am guided into withdrawal, in the sense of: I remain standing before it, without intervening. Then the situation is lifted into a greater connection. Then it can remain as it is, for what is happening is no longer personal. The greater fate is taking the whole matter into its service. Then we can see the heavy things more lightly somehow, and face them.

It is quite clear that it is a great relief for the client if we do not intervene in their special fate. This is basically all I have to say about that.

The couple relationship

HELLINGER: But back to the couple relationship. We do not just marry one person. The relationship goes to our partner and to their family and to the fate that comes with it. It goes to our partner's limitations and options, all at once. What this entails only shows up slowly in the course of the relationship. When we face this, we experience the couple relationship as a process of dying. Something superfluous falls away. Something from the past or something illusionary falls away. And after each marital argument both partners experience themselves purified from an illusion.

Once a man visited his friend, and the friend opened the door, beaming. The man asked his friend why he looked so happy. He replied: "I had an argument with my wife." "And this is why you are beaming now?" "Yes," he said, "afterwards it's so beautiful." That's also possible.

The entanglements in a couple relationship only emerge slowly. For instance, one of them wants to leave, because he or she is following a family member, or this person wants to take something on in the place of a family member. The children also see this, and then they get caught in this fate as well. We can't do anything about that. Then it takes this utmost humility: "I love you and that which guides me and you, in a special way." This is deep. This is greatness. This is the great love, the strong love.

This love also contains that we do not have to tolerate everything, as if it were the right thing.

There is, for instance, a concept of fidelity, which says: "You must be faithful to me," or, "I must be faithful to you." No, I don't have to. I must be true to the greater that guides me and you.

Demanding faithfulness, we sometimes hold the other captive. We demand loyalty to ourselves, instead of to something greater.

Where the greater remains seen, the relationship remains trustworthy. It can be relied upon in its depth, whatever may come. This is the big difference.

These were my final words. All the best to you.

Resonance

Recordings from workshops in Bad Sulza

All children are good – and so are their parents

The hidden love

HELLINGER: This thought, "All children are good, and so are their parents," may perplex some of you. How is this possible? The dimensions of this heading reach very deeply. For it says at the same time that we were good as children, and are still good to this day. It says that our parents are also good, because they were children, that they were good children, and still are good now, as parents.

I want to say something about the background of this sentence, apart from the superficial talk. When we say: "But the child did that, and the parents did this and that," they did, yes, but why? Out of love.

I will elucidate this in its depth now, and I will also do exercises with you that will help you to feel in your soul what it means to be really good. The conclusion is of course – I make this preemptive statement that all human beings are good the way they are. And furthermore, that people are good for the very reason that they are as they are. So that therefore we must not worry about ourselves or about our children or about our parents, whether they are good or bad. It is just our gaze that is dimmed sometimes, so that we don't see where we are good, where the children are good, where their parents are good.

So I want to clarify this first in an overview, before we begin to feel our way into it.

The spiritual field

Through family constellations it came to light that we are all embedded in a greater system, in a family system. Not only our

83

parents and their siblings belong to it, but also the grandparents, great-grandparents and the ancestors. There are more people who belong to this system because they were important for it in a special way, like for instance earlier partners of our parents or grandparents. In this system all members are directed by a shared power. This power follows certain laws.

This family system is a spiritual field. Within this spiritual field – as one can experience it through family constellations – everyone is in resonance with everyone else. Sometimes this field is in disorder. The disorder in a field comes about when someone who belongs to it was excluded or rejected or forgotten. These excluded or forgotten persons are in resonance with us, and they bring themselves to our attention in the present. In this field the all-encompassing law is: *Everyone who belongs to it, has the same right to belong*. Nobody can be excluded, no matter what.

Nobody is lost to this field. Everyone keeps on having effects on this field. If someone is excluded, regardless of the reasons, this person will be represented by another family member. Under the influence of this field, via this resonance, another family member will be chosen to represent the excluded person. Then this family member, a child for instance, behaves strangely. Perhaps the child will become addicted, or ill, or aggressive or a criminal. Perhaps he or she even becomes a murderer, or schizophrenic, anything is possible. But why? Because this person looks with love at an excluded person. Through their behavior this person forces us to look at the excluded person, with love. This so-called bad, even terrible, behavior is love for someone who was excluded from this field.

Now, looking at this child and worrying about him, and trying to change him, doesn't work anyway, as you know. Greater powers are at work here. We better look at this field to which we belong, together with this child, with the eyes of this child, until, under the guidance of the child, we actually look there where the excluded person is waiting for us. This person needs us to look at him or her and take him or her back into our soul, into our heart, into our family, into our group, perhaps even into our people and nation.

So, all children are good if we let them be good. This means, when we, instead of only looking at them, look where they look with love.

Now the great experience in family constellations is that instead of worrying about these children or other persons, thinking about their impossible behavior, we look at the excluded people with them and take them back into our family system. As soon as this person or these people are once again included in the soul of the parents and in the family and the group, the child heaves a sigh of relief, and can finally be free from the entanglement.

Once we know this, we can wait until we know where this child's behavior takes us as parents or as other family members. If we go there with the child, and take the other person along with us, the child is freed from behaving and feeling like someone else.

And who else is freed? We are, as parents or other family members. Suddenly we change, we feel richer, because now we have given a place inside us to something that was excluded. Everyone can behave differently now, relating fully to present life. With more love, with more ease, with more tolerance, beyond our cheap distinction of good and bad, which goes so smoothly with the assumption that we are better and the others are worse, even though the others whom we see as bad are just loving in a different way. When we look with them, where they love, the way they love, our distinctions between good and bad come to an end.

Another conclusion is of course that our parents are good and that behind anything that we perhaps want to object to in them, a different love is at work. This love does not go to us, though, but elsewhere, there where they looked as children, to someone whom they want to return to our family. When we begin to give these excluded people room in us, we also look in the same direction as our parents, there where their love goes. Suddenly we find ourselves in a completely different situation, and we learn what real love means.

Everything

Before we do an exercise, I will read you a little text from a book of mine that I still treasure, called: *Truth in Motion*. In this book there is a small text that condenses what I just explained, on a philosophical level. The text is called "Everything."

Everything can only be everything because it is connected to everything. Everything is connected to everything else. Nothing can be separate. Separation in this sense is connected with everything - everything is present in it. Therefore at the same time I am everything as well. Everything cannot be everything without me, and I cannot be without everything else.

What does this mean with regard to the way I live, to the way I feel, to the way I am? In each human being I see all human beings, and therefore I see me in them, too. And inside me I also sense all other human beings, each one as he or she is. In every other human being all human beings meet me, and I meet them all in each one of them.

How then could I reject anything in them without at the same time rejecting myself in them? How can I rejoice in them without being happy about myself in them? How could I wish others well without also wishing myself and all other people well? How can I love myself without loving all other people as well?

When we see everyone in everyone, we also see ourselves in them, we meet ourselves in them, we find ourselves in them. When we hurt others, we hurt ourselves. When we help others, we also help ourselves. When we withhold something from others, we withhold it from ourselves. And when we diminish them, we diminish ourselves. Who really loves, loves them all.

When we really love others, we love them all. Loving your neighbor is therefore loving all there is, including loving ourselves. This is the pure love, and the fulfilled love, because in everything it has everything, especially also itself.

Greatness

In the end, resonance means: "I love everyone." When I am in discord with someone or reject someone, I fall out of resonance with the whole, and I cannot evolve in resonance with the whole.

What is the solution? Everything I reject I take into my heart. This is the way to the love for all and everything. Through this love I become great. What does great mean here? I acknowledge that I am the same as all other people, and they are the same as me. For then I am connected with the whole, and through the whole I am great.

Meditation 1:
At whom does our illness look?

Now you can close your eyes. I will do a little meditation with you, in which you feel for yourselves what resonance means and what effect it has inside us.

Go into your body and sense where something hurts, where something is ill, where something does not work well. Obviously, what hurts or does not function well is in dissonance with our body. We lie down next to this pain, next to this illness, next to this organ, and we feel with the illness, with this organ, with this pain, where their gaze goes. What is this illness in resonance with? With which person that was perhaps rejected or forgotten or demonized or judged?

We wait until we can enter this movement, until we resonate, and perhaps we suddenly see where the gaze of the illness goes. For instance, to a child who died young or that was stillborn, or aborted or given away. Or to someone whom we judged as a criminal, with whom we want nothing to do, and with whom our family wants nothing to do any more. We look at this person as one of us and we say to this person, together with the illness: "Now I see you. I am like you. You are like me. Now I give you a place in my soul and in my family. Now you are with us again, one of us. You are no better and no worse before a greater power, before which we are like chess figures, with which this power plays in different ways. We acknowledge you are like us and we are like you."

Perhaps there are still more people we can also go to, whom we rejected, with whom we are angry, where we incurred guilt, or who injured us, and we say to everyone: "Yes." We sense what changes in our body, in our soul, and in our love.

Meditation 2:
At whom did we look as children?

This was a first step to develop a sense of what resonance means in the end. What it does inside us, and how we can experience something completely different through resonance, something towards which we had been closed before.

Now to some conclusions. With them we can continue the exercises. Close your eyes again.

You look at yourselves as children, how you behaved as children. Sometimes in a way that your parents worried about you, that they perhaps thought: "There's something not right with the child. How can he behave like this? Why is she so withdrawn? Why does he have so much fear? Why does she get so angry, so

88

impatient? Why does he not want to learn? Why does she want to give up, as if everything has become hopeless?"

As always, now you look at this child that you once were, and you feel very gently into the soul of this child: "Where did you look as a child, when you felt like this and felt that way? Where did the secret love go? With whom were you in deep resonance? Which person or persons wanted to bring themselves to your attention, so they would finally be seen and loved?"

You can say to your father or mother or both or also to others: "Please, look there with me, with love." Then you can acknowledge how much you loved as a child. Different than what was expected, but deeply in contact with someone who was not allowed to belong. You feel how good you were and are.

Okay, this was the second step.

Meditation 3:
At whom did your parents look as children?

Now we go a step further. Are you still with me? This goes deep, I know. But it makes us rich and wide. You can close your eyes again.

Now we look at our parents. Perhaps there were things we were at loggerheads with as children. We wished they would have been different. Now we look at them as they were as children, and where they looked as children. At whom did they look, who was excluded or forgotten? With whom were they in resonance? With whom are they perhaps still in resonance? How did they become the way they are, through this resonance, through this deep secret love? Now we look at this person or these persons with them, with their love, and we love these persons like our parents loved them as children, even though most of this was unconscious, this deep movement went towards someone whom they wanted to bring home.

We allow these persons to also bring themselves to our attention. We look at them and we say to them: "Yes, I see you. I also give you a place in my heart, with love."

Meditation 4:
At whom was our partner looking as a child?

Now we still go another step further in the same way. Close your eyes again, if you like, and look at your partner or another person who is close to you, with whom you are, and want to remain, connected. Perhaps you are uncomfortable about one or another behavior of this person.

Now allow yourself to look where this person looks with this behavior. At which excluded and perhaps rejected and condemned person? You look with your partner or another close person to where he or she looks, with love.

All this is a way to begin the practice of love for all. Can you feel how something changes in our soul through this? How we grow when we allow ourselves to open up to this movement?

Meditation 5:
At whom are our own children looking?

Now we still take one more step. You can close your eyes once more.

Look at your children, or, if you don't have any, at the children of relatives. Especially at those about whom you worry or who are ill or behave unfriendly. Look with them where they look with their behavior or with their illness. Which person wants to be seen and recognized in them? With whom are they in loving resonance? You look there with them, until you also see this person or these persons, suddenly perhaps, as if awakened from a deep dream, to suddenly see.

The love of all

Can anyone still doubt that all children are good? We as children? Our parents as children? Our partners as children? And our children as well? All are good.

This is the love of all. It expresses itself in something quite simple. That we look at all human beings, and give them a place in our heart.

There is an inner attitude that goes with this. It is a beautiful sentence: "Be merciful like my father in heaven. He lets the sun shine over the good and the bad, and he lets the rain fall equally over the just and the unjust." Why? He is in resonance with them all.

The family soul

What comes to light in this work in terms of new insights is that we are all embedded in a greater soul, in a family soul. Then we also speak of a spiritual field, even though this term does not explain much in this connection here. But there are other connections in which it plays a big role.

The spiritual field is a field in which something is conscious, aware. It is knowing. In this field there is a movement that wants to bring back together what was separated. This movement is a conscious movement. This field has a clear aim to bring something into conscious awareness. Therefore I prefer to rather speak of a great soul, of a shared soul, of a common soul in which we experience ourselves as connected with all who belong.

Through a range of behaviors it is brought to our awareness that there are matters we need to look at. If we do, something is brought into order in this field. It restores itself because excluded or forgotten people come into our awareness. This also has effects on the soul of the individual who wants to connect the separated. The individual is relieved from disorder.

These movements are movements of love. Many ways of behaving, especially in children, that give us cause for concern, are often deep movements of love that want to bring something to our attention that needs to be put in order. When their parents take notice of that and restore this order in themselves, then the whole family soul receives new strength. Above all, nobody needs to bring something forgotten or excluded to our attention any more, through ways of behaving that are distressing. All gain a greater degree of freedom from entanglement.

Bringing hidden love to light

What often comes to light through the behavior of children, even if it is rather difficult to deal with, reveals itself as something that is needed in the system. But as it is so difficult, the others do not want to look at it. The child takes it on himself to help the others. The child looks with love at the excluded persons. Behind the behavior a hidden love is at work. In our work with difficult children we therefore do not look so much at the child, but rather *with* the child. We look where the child looks. Then a healing movement is set in motion that frees the child, because now the others are also looking there where they need to look. The child no longer has to look there in the place of the others, and therefore this child does not need to exhibit the stressful behaviors. This is the essential mode of proceeding in our endeavor to help children.

When we consider what happens with so many so-called "difficult" children, when they are treated and given medication, as if they were dysfunctional, we overlook their love. The truth is, they do something for others, for the big ones. Therefore the kind of help as we can experience it here is groundbreaking for children, and it opens new ways. But we can break new ground only if we do not continue with our superficial concentration on the children, but instead redirect our focus where the children have been drawn to, and what they want to achieve for the adults. Then the children are relieved of their burden.

The parents, and whoever else is involved, must change their focus. They must look at what until now they have not looked at. This initiates a growth process in the parents. When the parents are consciously taking on what the children had done subconsciously, the children can be free. Then as a family they can look at excluded people together, for the benefit of all involved.

The order in the family

This is systemic pedagogy, a completely different pedagogy. This is the secret of this work. It is a special way of helping people in their lives. Here I am helping children out of an entanglement, and I restore something in their family system to order.

The disorder in a family is always the same: Members who belong to the family are excluded. There are also people who belong to the family that the family is not aware of, for instance the victims of family members. Where someone from a family was involved in the death of others, perhaps in a deliberate way, then these dead people belong to the family system. They are present in it. They have an effect, and they often bring themselves to attention through a child. Then this child looks to them. If the adults do not look there also, the child's behavior remains a puzzle to them. Those whom it really concerns must look. Then the disorder can move into order again.

Order is also about completion. Excluded people must be re-included. This is what I keep in mind above all in my work, now and in the future. It is help for the soul, for the dead and living, help for life in a comprehensive way. It opens new perspectives for other connections. With them in mind it becomes easier to help children and their parents.

The knowing love

Among the deeper causes that create difficulties for children is the idea that they can and may do something for their parents or their ancestors. This leads to endless problems for children and their parents. To understand this, one must know something about the distinction between the different consciences.

The good and the bad consciences

We sense our conscience as good conscience and as bad conscience, as guilt and innocence. Many are of the opinion that this has something to do with good and bad. But this is not so. It has something to do with our ties to the family and the separation from it. Everyone knows instinctively what he or she must do to be allowed to belong, through the help of their conscience. A child knows instinctively what he or she must do in order to belong to the family. If the child behaves accordingly, he or she has a good conscience. So, good conscience means: I feel that I have the right to belong.

If the child deviates from this, or if we deviate, we have the fear that we might lose our belonging. This fear is called bad conscience. Bad conscience means: I am afraid I might have lost my right to belong.

This conscience differs from group to group. It even differs from person to person. Therefore we have a different conscience concerning our father than concerning our mother, and a different one at work than at home. So, our conscience changes all the time, because our perception of what we need to do in order to belong differs according to different groups and to different circumstances.

With the help of our conscience we distinguish those who belong to us from those who don't. Through tying us to our family, our conscience distances us from others, and affirms separation from others. Therefore through our conscience we have feelings of rejection towards other people and groups, because these feelings have to do with belonging and not really with good and bad.

This is one kind of conscience, the conscience we can feel. Through this conscience we distinguish between good and bad, but always in connection to a particular group.

Entanglement

But now there is also a hidden conscience, an archaic, collective conscience. This conscience follows other laws than the conscience we can feel. This collective conscience is a conscience of the group. It takes care that everything is in order in the group, in the larger family.

The first law in this order is that everyone who belongs has the same right to belong. This is the basic law. But with the conscience that we feel, we exclude some people from our family. Those whom we see as bad, and also those we are afraid of. We exclude them because we think they are dangerous for us.

So now we have a conflict of consciences. The conscience that we feel and through which we exclude people is judged by the other conscience, which says that nobody can be excluded. Then under the conscience that we don't feel, someone is condemned to imitate a person who is excluded, but this person is not aware of imitating someone. This is entanglement.

So we can understand that the children who, in our view, behave strangely, or appear suicidal or addicted or whatever, have this special task of being connected to an excluded person, having to imitate their burdens. These children are entangled with such a person. Therefore we cannot help them, unless others in the family also look at the excluded person and take them (back) into the family and into their hearts. When this has happened, the children are free from the entanglement.

To help such children, others in the family who are still upset about someone or reject someone must turn to this person with love and take them back into the family.

This is the background for many difficulties of children, and the concerns parents have regarding their children.

Blind love

Now there is still another law in this conscience. It also leads to difficulties for children. This law says that the former members who belonged to the family earlier on have priority over those who came into the family later. This means there is an order of priority. This order of priority must be obeyed.

Many children assume they are entitled to do something for their parents, in order to help them. But this is an offense against this law. Then under the influence of this conscience the child says to the mother or the father an inner sentence, such as: "I take this on for you." "I will atone for you." "I will die for you." "I become ill for you." All of this comes from love, but from a blind love. This will lead to behaviors like addiction, suicidal tendencies, and to aggressive behavior. These behaviors and these ways of endangering their own lives have to do with the attempt to take something on for the parents. This offends the order of priority and the order of love.

Orders restored

Once we know about these orders, we can restore them. This means, the parents or others whom it may concern own up to the consequences of their behavior. Then the child is free: he or she no longer has to take something on for others.

Offenses against this order of priority are punished by this conscience. This means, any child who tries to take something on for the parents or other earlier family members will fail. No attempt to take something on for parents or for other earlier family members will be successful. It is doomed to fail, and that means failure for all. We must know that. We must be clear about that. Therefore we lead the children out of this situation. We first look at the parents, and we let the parents solve the problem. Then the children are freed from it. As soon as the parents have resolved the matter for themselves, the children can be peaceful, and they feel secure.

These are the basic laws we need to keep in mind and in our inner understanding, whenever we want to help difficult children.

Fate

In this connection I would like to say something about guilt. Not in a moral sense, far be it from me. But often we feel guilty in the sense that someone suffered because of us. In the case of an abortion, for example, parents have a feeling of guilt. Or a mother may have feelings of guilt when as a consequence of a difficult birth a child suffers ongoing damage.

There are two ways of dealing with such guilt. One way is to feel guilty. Feeling guilty means, I am not looking at the person I have harmed. When I feel guilty I look at myself. I regret something and I think I should have acted differently. Then I have these feelings of guilt.

Feelings of guilt are a substitute for action. Those who feel guilty don't do anything. They remain passive. Others in a similar situation take action.

There is a good way to deal with guilt. We look at what happened, the way it happened, and we say: "I agree to it as it was.

I agree to the consequences, to all consequences, whatever will come of it." In that we have no feelings of guilt. We gain the strength to do something, the strength to do something good. With this action the guilt is lifted in a good way.

When we feel guilty, there is something else to consider. Behind it is an arrogation. We assume we had been free to do something in one way or in another.

Now we look beyond the dead about whose death we feel guilty. We imagine they are lying there before us. Then we look far beyond them, at their fate which is greater than us. We ask fate to take care of them, and also of us. Do we sense the difference?

Then these dead have a point of reference where they can find peace. There they are all in safe care – all to the same extent.

Meditation:
Beyond good and bad

HELLINGER *to a woman whose sister and father are schizophrenic:* Close your eyes. Now you look at God. But not at the one whom many fear. Look at the greater one, this greater power that guides everything, for the better, when we acknowledge it. This means, we take care not to put ourselves into this power's place. You look constantly in this direction, without being distracted by your schizophrenic family members. You look at this power with love, constantly and without moving.

When the schizophrenic ones look at you, it does not help them for you are always looking into the same direction. Suddenly they are looking in the same direction as you.

HELLINGER: How are you?
WOMAN: I feel my heart very much now.
HELLINGER: Okay, all the best to you.

To the group: We can also help in this way, quite simply, by going into an inner movement. The exercise I did with her overcomes the widespread fear that there are good powers and bad powers, that one lot of powers is in conflict with the others, and that we must protect ourselves against the bad ones. We protect ourselves by looking beyond them, to that power that takes everything equally into its service. We can remain undeterred by those who are seen as belonging to the bad ones, whatever they may say or do or whatever is said about them. When we just look at this one power, in this direction, this has a magnetic effect. Suddenly they also look there, and they heave a sigh of relief.

The Other Way of Telling

Recordings from a workshop in Duisburg for people with speech problems

Speech problems

Behind many speech problems there is an unresolved conflict in the family. For instance perhaps someone in the family was not supposed to be there or to speak up, or someone was kept a secret or was given away. Or because two people opposed each other irreconcilably, for instance a perpetrator and his victim. As a consequence, a descendant often represents both at once, and therefore is unable to let each one speak alone. Then this person begins to stutter.

So stuttering often has a similar systemic background to schizophrenia. Whilst in schizophrenia the unresolved conflict is expressed in the confusion, it shows through speech in the stuttering person. The solution for the stuttering person is often the same as for the schizophrenic person. The still unreconciled family members are placed opposite each other until they acknowledge one another and reconcile. When it comes to light where the real conflict lies, the people with the speech problem or the schizophrenia can leave it where it belongs and free themselves from it.

Stuttering can also have other backgrounds. We can often observe that people who stutter often look sideways before the stuttering begins. This means, they look at an internalized image, or more precisely, at an internalized person of whom they are afraid, and before whom they begin to stutter. When, in a constellation, stutterers can openly face such a person and honor him or her until the other side reciprocates and shows love in return, the stutterers can look into such a person's eyes and clearly say what they feel and what they are asking from that person.

Sometimes the stuttering and other speech problems hide a secret that wants to come to light -- a child nobody knew about, for instance. When this secret is revealed and clearly seen, the former obstacle clears the path to fluent speech.

The right word

I would like to say something about speaking. What happens when we say something? What effect does saying the right word have? When a child says the word "mama" for the first time, do you feel what this means? Do you notice the difference from the earlier state? What does this word "mama" do to the mother? She changes. Something changes through this one word, uttered by the child. Something also changes in the child when he or she succeeds in saying this word. The relationship from mother to child and from child to mother is changed. This word creates a new reality. In this word a new kind of relationship celebrates its success. When someone says the familiar form of you (du, tu, ti, ty; a form existing in most European languages) to a person for the first time, something is changed.

And what happens to things when we name them the right way? Often we think about a connection for a long time, and we cannot grasp it. But as soon as we can, it concentrates and condenses in a truth that is spoken in one word. Only what has been grasped can also be said, and it has a special effect. It changes something. This is the difference from blabbering. Those words do not change anything. To the contrary, they distract from true comprehending. When something is grasped it can also be said. Such a word has power.

In family constellations, quite often a word is due, or a sentence, sometimes just *one* word, just *one* sentence. This word and this sentence have the power to change something. Only when the helper has grasped which word can turn something around, and he puts it in the client's mouth, so to speak, so that it can be said, then something changes. This word is creative.

The great words come out of silence. They need time to ripen, until they can be ripe fruit that falls from the tree of knowledge. They are words of insight.

When someone is hindered in speaking, then this person is also hindered in relating to others, especially – such is my image – in the relationship to mother and father.

Something else needs to be kept in mind here. A thing that is not named, not correctly named, cannot come into its fullness. Let's take a simple word, such as the word "rose." When we have grasped it and said it, the rose is different in its being. It is no longer the same as before. In its word, an uncompleted thing, an uncompleted relationship, an uncompleted situation is taken along towards something greater. It is ensouled through this word.

When we let this sink in, we become cautious when we speak. The right saying leads further at the right time.

When we consider that, we pay attention to the effect a word will have. Before we say it, we listen inside to know the effect it has – in our own soul and in other people's souls.

Often, when I work with someone, I do not allow any speaking. I interrupt the urge to speak. What is the effect? It prepares the right word and the essential speaking.

There's another distinction here. What do words about problems do, and what do words towards action do, or towards a solution or reconciliation? How different is their effect?

When we allow people to talk about their problems, we often prevent the resolving word from coming.

The refusal

HELLINGER *to a client*: What is your issue?
CLIENT: It's about my daughter.
HELLINGER: What is the matter with her?

CLIENT: She speaks poorly.

HELLINGER: How old is she?

CLIENT: Six years. She has a great...

HELLINGER *interrupts him*: No. What will I do now?

CLIENT: Set up her and her mother.

HELLINGER: Exactly. You learned fast.

HELLINGER: We try it out. We don't know yet. But I will begin with this.

Hellinger lets the participant choose the representative for the mother. Hellinger chooses the representative for the daughter and places her opposite the mother. The participant says that his wife is also present. Hellinger gets her to sit next to her husband.

After a while Hellinger turns the mother around.

HELLINGER *to the mother's representative*: How is this, better or worse?

REPRESENTATIVE OF THE MOTHER: Better.

HELLINGER *to the mother*: Where is the problem?

She nods towards the representative of the daughter.

HELLINGER: Where? We can see this here in the constellation.

MOTHER: I don't see it that way.

HELLINGER: Then I will interrupt here.

To the representatives: You can sit down again.

To the group: Here we gain another important insight about speech problems. The child can't be helped when the person for whom the child does it refuses cooperation.

The interruption

PARICIPANT: My question is: Was the interruption in the constellation an intervention and the beginning of a change in understanding?

HELLINGER: You have seen this correctly. That it was an interruption was only the surface. It was something that prepared a change.

To the group: This here is hard work. It demands high concentration, also from you. Perhaps also re-thinking.

Continuation

HELLINGER *again to the mother*: I will continue with you.

To the group: Earlier on, when I turned her representative around, the child began to shake. The child fears for her mother.

To the mother: Is she not a dear child?

The mother wipes away a tear.

HELLINGER *to the group*: It is quite clear, the child's problem has nothing to do with the relationship to the child's mother. Perhaps it has something to do with the mother's family of origin.

To the mother: Do you know what the child's fear is?

The mother shakes her head.

HELLINGER: That you will kill yourself.

MOTHER: For whom?

She begins to cry and moves her hand in a defensive gesture.

HELLINGER *to the group*: Did the word I said to her reach her soul?

105

After a while to the mother: I think I still have to wait until we can continue to work. Okay?

She nods.

HELLINGER *to the group*: Now I have turned the soil a bit, and I wait until the little plant grows a bit more.

The solution

HELLINGER *to the mother*: Now I will work with you once more. It is the last chance.

Hellinger gets her to sit next to him, together with her husband.

HELLINGER *to the group*: When a couple is separated, that also leads to disturbances.
To the mother: What did I tell you this morning? What is your child's fear, and why does she shake?
MOTHER: Because I want to go. But I don't want to go.
HELLINGER: Because she's afraid that you will kill yourself. This is the depth of the situation. What happened in your family of origin?
MOTHER: Nothing happened in my family of origin.
HELLINGER: Of course. Nothing. Not even a child came.

The mother laughs, and then begins to cry.

HELLINGER *to the couple*: Was one of you married before?

The woman shakes her head, the man nods.

HELLINGER *to the husband*: Were there children from this relationship?

106

The husband signals no.

HELLINGER: So the problem lies in her family.

To the group: I will do a simple test to see if it is her mother's line or in her father's line.

Hellinger chooses a man and a woman as the representatives for the mother's father and mother, and he sets them up.

The father looks away, the mother looks ahead. Hellinger observes the two representatives.

HELLINGER: It is primarily in the line of the mother.

As he says this, the child's mother looks quite affected.

HELLINGER *to the mother*: What was in your mother's family?

MOTHER *breathes deeply and moans*: I know that my mother had a miscarriage before me. At the time she had no relationship with my father as yet. She had a great love whom she was not allowed to marry, and of whom she still says to this day, that she gets weak in the knees when she sees him. My mum was somehow never there.

HELLINGER: This is just foreground. What happened in her family?

MOTHER: I know little about my mother's family. She has a half-sister, who was only presented to the family when she wanted to marry. She came into the family as a half-sister. She is the oldest sister. There are three sisters, my mother is the one in the middle, if one takes the half-sister as the oldest. She was born out of an affair my grandfather had. This half-sister has given a baby up for adoption, to America. This is what I know about my mother's family.

HELLINGER: This is a lot. Who wants to commit suicide in this family? First, the grandfather, next the half-sister, thirdly, the child who was given away.

The mother cries.

MOTHER: I always had the feeling I have no place.

HELLINGER: Exactly. But those without place are your mother's half-sister, and her child, and the half-sister's mother. None of them have a place in this family.

MOTHER: The mother of my half-sister is not there either, that's right.

HELLINGER *to the group*: Now I will begin a long way back, independently of her.

Hellinger chooses representatives for the client's grandfather, her grandmother, the mother of her mother's half-sister, her mother's half-sister, and for the half-sister's child who was given away. He places them all next to each other.

Hellinger asks the client to place the representatives. As she hesitates, he asks her to wait a little longer. Then he places the grandfather away from the others.

HELLINGER *to the grandfather*: Are you feeling better or worse now?

GRANDFATHER: I feel better.

HELLINGER: Exactly.

To the client: He is the first suicidal person.

Now the client begins to set the representatives up.

When the client has placed the grandmother and the grandfather, Hellinger takes the grandmother in the direction of her gaze. He places her far away.

HELLINGER *to the grandmother*: How do you feel here, better or worse?

GRANDMOTHER: Better.

HELLINGER *to the mother*: She is the second suicidal person.

Hellinger takes the grandmother back to her place in the constellation. Now the client is also placing the others: the first wife of the grandfather and the half-sister opposite, the grandmother behind the grandfather, but with her gaze away from him. The child who was given up stands far away from the others, looking into the distance.

Now Hellinger places the client and a representative for the client's daughter. Both stand away and opposite each other. The client looks to the floor. Hellinger gets another woman to lie with her back on the floor in front of the client, representing a dead child. The client speaks.

MOTHER: Before she was lying there, I wanted to curl up and make myself tiny.

HELLINGER *to the group*: Do you notice how her babbling took away the power and the seriousness?

The client nods.

HELLINGER: This is a dead child of yours.

MOTHER *turning to Hellinger*: Yes, there is one.

HELLINGER: Exactly, and there it is.

After a while to the client's daughter: Lie down next to the child.

HELLINGER *to the daughter*: How do you feel there, better or worse?

DAUGHTER: Better.

HELLINGER *to the group*: We could see how she heaved a sigh of relief.

To the daughter: Look at your mother. Say to her: "I will die for you."

DAUGHTER: I will die for you.

After a while the mother kneels between the two children and cries. She takes both children by the hand. Hellinger intervenes and gets the daughter to stand again. The mother strokes the dead child, embraces the child and draws the child close to her. The two embrace tenderly.

HELLINGER *to the daughter*: How are you now?

DAUGHTER: Quite good.

HELLINGER: Exactly. Now you need not step in between.

The mother is still embracing her dead child with great tenderness.

HELLINGER *after a while to the daughter*: How is it now for you?

DAUGHTER: Still very good.

HELLINGER: Now you are out of this.

To the mother/client and the representatives: We can leave it here.

To the group: What was earlier is now not so important any more. Something that was nearer is very important, even though the other matter was also significant.

To the client/mother: Can I leave it here?

MOTHER *obviously relieved*: Yes.

HELLINGER: Okay. That's that.

To the group: In family constellations we can receive the important hints immediately, if we observe precisely what goes on. When the daughter stood in the constellation, she briefly looked to the floor.

To the client: When I placed you, you did not look at the others, but immediately to the floor. Through that it was clear: Here was the essential matter.

To the group: We do not need to search for what exactly happened. What for? It is none of my business. I wanted to find a solution for the daughter.

To the client: Okay?

She nods.

HELLINGER *to the group*: There is the great danger that afterwards some go to the client to ask her what it was or even to comfort her. These are the weak helpers, the weakling helpers, one could say. The strange thing is: When they do this, they feel better. Better than me, for instance, and better than the client.

But how much responsibility are they taking on? None at all. They feed on their comforting others. This is a kind of vampirism. If we look at it closely, it is vampirism. It's just that the teeth are hidden.

Are you crazy?

HELLINGER *to a young man*: I will work with you.

The young man wears a small knitted cap. He sits down next to Hellinger, bends forward and looks to the floor.

HELLINGER *after a while*: Are you – crazy?

The young man looks to Hellinger and says: No. Then he looks to the floor again. After a while he moves his eyes to the right and to the left and fidgets around with his hands. Then a smirk comes over his face. He briefly looks to Hellinger and then he quickly turns his head back again. Laughing in the group.

The young man keeps on grinning and shakes his head.

HELLINGER *after a while to the group*: He is crazy.

As the group is laughing, Hellinger puts a stop to it.

HELLINGER *seriously*: Of course, he is crazy.

The young man is also serious again.

HELLINGER *to the young man*: How many people and helpers have you fooled already?

The young man looks around furtively and grins. Hellinger grins too.

HELLINGER *to him*: I will leave it here for the moment. Okay?

The young man goes back to his place.

HELLINGER *to the group*: What did I do now? I have stripped him of his power.

The young man laughs as if he has been caught. The group laughs too.

"I am one of you"

The young man comes back without his little cap.

HELLINGER *to the group*: He has taken his fool's cap off today. This is really wonderful.

To him: You did well. Sit up straight. Still a bit more straight.

The young man, who sat severely bent over before, is now straightened up.

HELLINGER: This suits you well.
To the group: I will do a little bit of education.

The young man laughs.

HELLINGER *to the organizer*: I had asked you to find out if he was adopted?
ORGANIZER: He has been a foster child since he was three.
HELLINGER *to him*: What about your parents?
YOUNG MAN *stuttering*: My parents were alcoholics then. How they are going these days, I don't know.
HELLINGER: Do you know where they are?
YOUNG MAN: No.
HELLINGER: *to the group*: Well, just for you as an exercise. If he is with his foster parents and he wants to be with his parents and love them: What is the reaction?

To the young man: Do you think you could do that?

He thinks for a long time and shakes his head.

HELLINGER: Exactly. No.
To the group: He gets into a conflict between the foster parents on the one hand and his parents on the other. What else is left for him but to stutter?

To him: Can you understand what I am saying? Shall we take the matter on?

He nods.

Hellinger chooses representatives for the foster parents and for his own parents, and he places them opposite each other. Then he places the young man in between them. He looks to the floor.

HELLINGER *to the group*: He stands there as if he feels guilty.
To him: Perhaps you think you caused bad luck for your parents. What were they supposed to do with you?

He keeps on looking to the floor. Hellinger takes him to his parents. He stands before them with clenched fists, but he does not look at them.

HELLINGER *to the group*: Look at his hands. There you see the aggression. What goes on in a child who was taken away from his parents at age three? He becomes angry.

The young man takes a step back.

HELLINGER: I get you to say a difficult sentence.

He nods.

HELLINGER: "For your sake, I make room." Look at them as you speak.
YOUNG MAN *fluently*: For your sake I make room.
HELLINGER: He can say this without any stuttering?
To him: Say it once more.

YOUNG MAN: For your sake, I make room.

He slowly moves further back and looks to the floor.

HELLINGER: Look at your parents once more and tell them: "You remain my parents."
YOUNG MAN *fluently throughout*: You remain my parents.
HELLINGER: "In my heart I take you with me."
YOUNG MAN: In my heart I take you with me.

He is still looking to the floor.

HELLINGER *after a while*: Look at them once more and say: "But I miss you very much."
YOUNG MAN: But I miss you very much.

He clenches his fists again, lowers his head still further, and looks to the floor.

HELLINGER: *Tell them*: "I am only a child."
YOUNG MAN: I am only a child.
HELLINGER: "Without guilt."
YOUNG MAN: Without guilt.
HELLINGER: "You are the parents."
YOUNG MAN: You are the parents.
HELLINGER: Look at them.

He looks at them, lowers his head again and looks to the floor.

HELLINGER: Look at them and say, "Please."
YOUNG MAN: Please.

HELLINGER: Go with your movement. It is okay.

He goes towards them slowly and then throws his arms around his father. Both embrace lovingly. But his fists are still clenched. He stands next to his father and looks to the ground again.

HELLINGER *to him*: Look at your foster parents and say to them, "Here is my place."
YOUNG MAN: Here is my place.
HELLINGER: "Whatever it may cost me."
YOUNG MAN: Whatever it may cost me.
HELLINGER: "Here is my place."
YOUNG MAN: Here is my place.
HELLINGER *after a while to the father and the mother*: Now you say to them: "Thank you."
FATHER: Thank you.
MOTHER: Thank you.

The young man looks at the floor again. Then he stands behind his parents.

Hellinger chooses a woman and gets her to lie on the floor, on her back, in front of the parents.
 The mother looks to the son, away from the dead woman. Then she looks to her husband. They take each other's hands. The mother puts her head on her husband's shoulder and sobs. The father looks to the dead woman. The young man who still had his fists clenched, is now releasing them.

HELLINGER *after a while to the mother*: Tell your son: "You are innocent."

MOTHER *looks to the son*: You are innocent.

HELLINGER: "I am guilty."

MOTHER *very moved and with a weak voice*: I am guilty.

She looks at her son. He slowly walks towards her and then embraces her. The father embraces both of them. The young man has put his head between the parents, on their shoulders, and he embraces them tenderly and for a long time. After a while Hellinger releases him from the parents and asks him to step back and to kneel in front of them.

HELLINGER: Look at them and say: "Here I am only the child."

YOUNG MAN: Here I am only the child.

HELLINGER: "And I remain the child."

YOUNG MAN: And I remain the child.

HELLINGER *to the group*: When he went to his parents earlier on, he behaved as the big one. He has taken on a double load for them. The guilt is one load. This showed in the aggression in his fists. At the same time he is connected with the victim. This is the dynamic of schizophrenia, to be connected to both the perpetrator and the victim at once.

To the young man: Now you get out of that. You are only the child. The guilt remains where it belongs.

He looks to the floor again.

HELLINGER *to the group*: He looks to the victim for his mother. He initiated all of this. I relied on him. He knew it. He has taken the lead.

To the young man: Hello.

The young man laughs.

HELLINGER: Now you get out of this and you stand tall.

Hellinger leads him past the parents before the victim. He asks the parents to turn around.

HELLINGER *to the young man*: And now you turn away.

Hellinger turns him away from the victim, to the group.

HELLINGER: Have a look at the people.

He looks and is still serious.

HELLINGER *to the group*: He is as if in prison, and he does not quite have the courage as yet.

His face lightens up, and he laughs.

HELLINGER: Tell them: "I am one of you."
YOUNG MAN: I am one of you.

Loud laughing and applause from the group.

HELLINGER *as he still looks down*: You may as well look up.

He straightens up and looks ahead.

HELLINGER: Exactly. That's it then.
To the representatives: Thank you all.

To the representative of the dead woman who is still lying down:
How are you?
REPRESENTATIVE: I died.

She gets up slowly.

HELLINGER *to the group*: The dead woman is obviously a child of the parents.
To the young man: A sibling of yours. Give this sibling a place in your heart.

Erroneous ways of helping

HELLINGER: It is a part of the orders of helping that we do not take on the position of identification, that we do not take sides for a better or worse, or for a perpetrator or a victim. Above all, that we do not rise above the parents like a child.

The young man was in this assuming position in regard to his parents. Internally he said to them: "I will take it on for you." I guided him back into the position of the child. This has a special effect in the soul. Often children feel guilty when they withdraw from the superior position of someone who wants to do something for the parents, into the position of the child.

Helpers have to do the same thing. They must not want to help the parents like a child. Those who are desperately looking for solutions maneuver themselves into this assuming attitude.

What I am saying here is revolutionary, if you consider how far we can go astray when we believe we have to help and we're allowed to do so.

I once heard a sentence that sums it up: "Who has pity is accusing God."

The secret

HELLINGER *to a female client*: What is it about?

CLIENT: That two of my children learn to speak more clearly and correctly.

HELLINGER: How old are the children?

CLIENT: 3½, and 4½.

HELLINGER: What is the difficulty?

CLIENT: They don't speak clearly and correctly. They swallow letters.

HELLINGER *to the group*: I have difficulty understanding her. Did you have the same problem?

To the client: Who needs to speak more clearly?

CLIENT: I do.

They look at each other for a long time. Then she looks at the floor in front of her.

HELLINGER *as she wants to say something*: Stay there. Bear it. You are already at the scene. Keep on looking that way.

As she wants to turn to him: Stay there. Bear it.

She begins to cry.

HELLINGER *after a while*: And now say what it is about in that situation, clearly.

CLIENT *not clearly*: I want to be allowed to say what is going on.

HELLINGER: I did not understand a thing.

To the group: Did you understand it?

To the client: Say it with anger.

CLIENT: I want to say what the reality is.

HELLINGER: Speak the reality!

CLIENT *crying*: Let me talk! Listen to me!

HELLINGER You're not ready yet, to say it clearly. I interrupt it here. Okay?

She nods.

HELLINGER *to the group*: In any case, the children are unburdened. Earlier on in my life, when I was still young, I looked for solutions. I abandoned that a long time ago. I only bring something to light. That's all. Then I can lean back and let things take their course.

Continuation

HELLINGER *to the client*: I take this up once more with you. Has it become clear to you what the situation is?

CLIENT *not clearly*: It is about my parents and my grandfather, my mother's father.

HELLINGER: Can you speak a little more clearly?

Both laugh.

CLIENT: Yes. It is about my parents and my mother's father. That's it.

HELLINGER: What is it about them?

CLIENT *not clearly*: There is this discord.

HELLINGER: Sorry, I can't understand you.

Both laugh again.

CLIENT: There is this discord, that there is no concord. One works against each other.

HELLINGER *to the group*: If this were the real issue, she would have been able to speak clearly.

Hellinger looks over to her. She looks to the floor.

HELLINGER: What is the unspeakable secret?

She keeps on looking to the floor.

HELLINGER: Stay that way, exactly like that.

Hellinger gets a woman to lie down in front of her, where her gaze goes. The client is still sitting next to Hellinger. The client looks at this dead woman, mesmerized, without moving.

HELLINGER: Are your two children boys or girls?
CLIENT: A boy and a girl.
HELLINGER: The older child is?
CLIENT: A boy.

Hellinger chooses a representative for the boy and for the girl and places them opposite the dead woman.

The children look at the dead person, unwavering.

HELLINGER *to the client*: It appears as if the dead woman were a sibling of the two.

The client does not say a word and keeps on looking at the dead woman, still mesmerized. The son goes to the dead woman and kneels in front of her. Then he gets up and kneels down a bit further away.

HELLINGER *to the client as he sees that she wants to move*: Go with your movement.

She kneels by the side of the dead woman, who sobs, and she bends down to her, takes her into her arms, then looks across to her children and cries. She bends over the dead woman again, straightens up and looks across to the children. The daughter has withdrawn quite a bit and turned away. The son goes closer to the mother and holds her arm tightly. The daughter has left the stage, as if wanting to disappear completely.

HELLINGER: I interrupt it here.

The client sits down next to Hellinger again.

HELLINGER *to the client*: Do you know who the dead woman is?
CLIENT: Is it perhaps my child, that I lost?
HELLINGER: You lost a child?
CLIENT: Yes, I had a miscarriage.
HELLINGER: There must be more. There was a strange displacement. One of the children, the son, suddenly behaved like the father of the child.

The client cries and looks at the floor in front of her.

HELLINGER *to the group*: We can see that she sees the scene quite exactly. The soul is looking there. Something like this is always murder.

Long silence.

HELLINGER: Where is the murder?

CLIENT: I see my grandfather.

HELLINGER: What was happening?

CLIENT: I see my grandfather and a sister, my sister. I see this sister. I don't know her.

HELLINGER *to the group*: Now she talked fairly clearly -- this is remarkable.

To the client: You are on to something.

She cries and keeps on looking to the same spot.

CLIENT: My mother had a child who would have been my half-sister, and my grandfather has destroyed her.

HELLINGER: Destroyed?

CLIENT: He has strangled her, that is what I see.

HELLINGER: This is it, the unspeakable secret.

The client sobs loudly.

Hellinger asks the representative of the dead child to stand again, as the half-sister of the client. He places the client opposite her.

The client takes one step towards the dead half-sister and opens her arms invitingly. The half-sister looks to the side and moves backwards. The client takes one more step closer to her. The half-sister turns sideways.

HELLINGER *to the client, as she wants to go closer still*: Wait.

Hellinger chooses a representative for the grandfather and places him in front of the dead half-sister.

As soon as the grandfather stands in front of her, the half-sister sobs and moves backwards away from him and then turns away. She throws her hands up to her face, and sinks to her knees, sobbing loudly, and she bends forward grasping her upper arms with her hands. The client steps back farther.

Hellinger chooses a representative for the half-sister's mother and places her with the other two. The half-sister twists and turns, whilst still kneeling. The mother wants to touch her, but she is shaking with fear.

The mother steps back a little, covers her own face and turns away slowly. The child is constantly shaking, twisting and turning. She looks over to the grandfather. He stands there, unmoved.

Hellinger signals to the client to sit down again.

The child calms down somewhat. She looks pleadingly at the grandfather who remains unmoved. She starts sobbing, turns to him on her knees and lifts her hands towards him pleadingly. In the meantime the mother has turned away completely.

Hellinger asks the client to kneel next to her half-sister and to look at the grandfather together with her.

The client puts her arms around her half-sister, who reaches out for her hand and calms down.

Now Hellinger gets both of the client's children to kneel next to their mother. At this the grandfather moves back a bit.

The mother puts her left arm around her half-sister. With her right hand she holds her children. The half-sister has calmed down in the meantime. All four together look at the grandfather.

HELLINGER *to the client:* Say to the grandfather, "It was you."
CLIENT *with a loud and clear voice:* It was you.
HELLINGER: This was clear.

125

The client breathes deeply. She puts her right arm around her two children. Her daughter puts her arm around the mother. All four are in a tight embrace.

Now Hellinger places the client's mother next to the grandfather.

HELLINGER *to the mother*: You must look at it.

The client and her half-sister look at each other lovingly. Then the client looks lovingly at her children.

HELLINGER *after a while to the group*: Now everything is clear. The matter between grandfather and grandmother we need not solve.
To the client: Is it clear to you?

The client nods.

HELLINGER: Okay. Good.

The client sits next to Hellinger and shakes his hand, visibly moved.

HELLINGER *to the group*: What is the next step for her? – and for the helper? How could it continue? She and the helper must take the grandfather and the child's mother into their heart.

The client nods.

HELLINGER: And at the same time leave them with this child. This is the hard step.

Hellinger calls the representative of the grandfather over.

HELLINGER *to this representative*: In your inner image, bow to the real grandfather with respect.

He bows slowly.

HELLINGER: And now you straighten up, turn away, and you are yourself again.

The representative turns away and laughs with relief.

HELLINGER *to the group*: When someone has taken on such a heavy representation, we can get him out of that in this way. Then it is necessary. With the others who did not have such heavy representations it is not so necessary.

Helping out of weakness, helping out of strength

HELLINGER: I would like to say something about love. A great deal of love is weakness. Many love because they cannot bear something, because they cannot bear some other people and their fate. Therefore they became helpers.

A young child cannot bear what goes on in the family: what happens with the mother, with the father, with their fate, and with their guilt. Therefore this child wants to help. Then he or she takes something on for the father, for the mother, for others in the family – out of weakness. This person turns into a helper with love, but out of weakness.

Many adult helpers still help according to the pattern of such a child. There is something they cannot bear, and they try to change something. But not because the other person needs it. They take something on without respect for the other's greatness and fate, and also for their guilt.

A child grows when he or she learns to love with respect for the greater that guides the parents and also everything else.

Thus helpers also help differently once they have gained strength. They bear the fate of others. Then they can support others in a way that they can stand on their own two feet, often in a way that the other gives up helping out of weakness too. This would be the other love.

Helping in accord

I would like to say something else about helping. The way I proceed here can be compared to the work of a gardener. The gardener does what is needed at the moment, then he lets things grow without intervening. What I am doing here is, I walk those steps with the client that are needed at the moment, to serve his or her growth. I am in awe of the laws of growth and development.

If you compare this with the other attitude, where someone says: "I will solve this for you," you can see that this person is acting like a technician who deals with some dead matter, and who is only satisfied when the thing is fixed.

I am trying to go with the laws of the soul. The main attribute of the gardener is the patience to wait for the right time for the fruit.

Reconciling opposites

I will add something about what is crazy. Crazy is someone who cannot bring something together. As a rule this means people who are opposed to each other. The crazy person must deal and get along with both sides, but cannot do so, because the two are in conflict with each other. Something unresolved is between them, such as between perpetrators and victims. Having to represent both sides, the person goes crazy. Usually this means, schizophrenic.

It is perhaps similar with speech disorders. So far it is a hypothesis. Someone's speech is in disarray, especially in stuttering, because two opposite people want to have their say at the same time, each one against the other. One wants to say something, but is not allowed to. One person wants something, the other is against it. This leads to stuttering, or some other kind of speech problem.

When I worked here, this image came to me. That the speech disorder can be lifted when those opposing each other on the soul level can be brought together and reconcile. Then the words can also reconcile and show themselves as belonging together, as a coherent whole.

The requirement for this is that something similar also takes place in the helpers. The helpers must also guide the opposing souls back together, in their soul.

Street Children

Recordings from a workshop in Mexico

Real life

HELLINGER: Often we imagine what a truly happy childhood would have to look like, and what would prepare us best for life. So, loving parents without any faults, always there for us, supporting us in every way and protecting us from any harm. How do these children fare in life? What do they know about the hardships of life, and the challenges it will pose to us? How resilient will they be? Will they be fit for life? When it is a matter of surviving even under great difficulties, they are often disadvantaged and fare poorly, compared to other children who had a tough childhood.

In Germany I sometimes compare university students to the little 6- to 7-year-old boys in Latin America who sell newspapers. How strong they already are, how self-reliant! At such a young age they already know to take responsibility for the livelihood of the family, and they contribute to it without a question. How much alertness and what inner strength!

I have the deepest respect for them. They know something about the hardships of life, and what it ultimately demands of us.

Example: "Please"

Hellinger asks a boy, about 13 years old, to come and sit next to him. He comes with his hands in his pockets, and sits down next to Hellinger, shy and clumsy.

HELLINGER *to this boy*: You are not yet used to something like this.

The boy is very moved and looks to the floor.

HELLINGER: Just look at me.

The boy sits leaning forward, with his upper body turned sideways by Hellinger, and from below he looks to him. Then he looks to the floor again.

HELLINGER: It's okay like this for me. Just look at me a bit.

Hellinger puts his hand on the boy's knee.

HELLINGER: When I look at you, I see that you have given up hope in other people. Obviously you have experienced many hard things.

The boy nods.

HELLINGER: I see it.

The boy looks to the floor again.

HELLINGER: Sometimes, in a dark night, people wait with great longing for the sun to rise again. After a dark night it is beautiful to see the sun shine again. Sometimes life is like that. And here, a new day is also dawning after a dark night. Shall we look out for the light? For the light that is for you?

The boy has been looking to the floor the whole time.

HELLINGER: Look at me again.

The boy looks towards Hellinger and smiles.

HELLINGER: I see you feel a little more hopeful. Tell me something about your life.

The boy sighs deeply and begins to cry. Hellinger puts his arm around him and holds him for a long time. The boy has put his head on Hellinger's chest. After a while as Hellinger releases his arm, the boy looks away from him, and to the floor. Hellinger draws him close again, the boy puts his head on Hellinger's chest of his own accord.

After a while the boy releases himself. He looks to the side again, and to the floor.

HELLINGER: Tell me something about your father and about your mother.
BOY: What should I say?
HELLINGER: Something about what you have experienced with your father and your mother.
BOY: I did not have a good relationship with my parents.
HELLINGER: What happened?
BOY: I ran away from home because I could not bear it any more.
HELLINGER: How old were you then?
BOY: 10 years old.
HELLINGER: Where did you go then?
BOY: On the street.

Hellinger waits a long time. For the whole time he has held his right hand between the boy's shoulder blades. The boy is still looking to the floor.

HELLINGER: So you know how to survive on your own.

A long break again.

HELLINGER: Do you visit your parents occasionally?
BOY: Yes, occasionally.

HELLINGER: Do you want to say something about that?

BOY: No.

HELLINGER: I will do a little exercise with you. Close your eyes. Imagine your parents, how they looked at you when you were born. How they took you as their child. They fed you. They helped you, and you were allowed to live with them. They did not have much, but they tried their best.

As a little child you looked at them with love. They were the only ones on whom you could rely. Then you began to grow up. You saw how hard it was for your parents. Perhaps you also saw that they did not have the means to feed you. Then perhaps you said to them inside: "I do not want to be a burden on you. Now I will look after myself. Then it will be easier for you." And so you went away. But occasionally you visit them. You say to them: "I have done it on my own. I was strong enough to do it on my own. But I miss you very much. Look at me with love."

After a while Hellinger withdraws his hand. The boy remains in the same position and looks to the floor. Then Hellinger puts his hand on the boy's hand. They remain this way for a long time.

HELLINGER *after a while*: How are you now?

The boy looks across to Hellinger.

BOY: Good.

HELLINGER: I will do one more thing for you. Yes?

The boy nods.

Hellinger chooses representatives for the father and the mother of the boy and places them next to each other, the mother to the left of the father. As the boy sees this, he puts his hand in front of his eyes. Hellinger places him in front of his parents.

HELLINGER *to the boy*: Imagine you have just come back from the street and you go home. Look at them.

All remain without motion for a long time. Then the mother takes a small step away from the father, then another little step and another. Doing this, she always looks to the floor.

After a while Hellinger chooses a representative and asks him to lie on the floor on his back in front of the mother. As he lies there, the mother takes a little step back, but keeps on looking at the dead man. Then she takes another little step back. The dead man looks at the mother the whole time. Then he looks at the boy. The mother quickly looks to the father, but he does not move. He always looks straight ahead.

After a while the mother goes on her knees and looks at the dead man. He looks back and forth between the mother and the son. He reaches one hand out to the boy, but then pulls it back, and begins to sob loudly. Meanwhile, the mother has gotten up again and has moved back several steps.

She puts her left hand to her heart. The father remains without any movement.

HELLINGER *after a while to the boy*: Do you know who the person on the floor could be?
BOY: Me.
HELLINGER: This is a dead person who is connected to your mother. Who could it be?
BOY: My aunt.
HELLINGER: What happened to her?
BOY: I don't know.

HELLINGER: Your mother looked to the floor. It shows that she looks at a dead person. It is possible that the dead person was a child of your mother's. Do you know anything about that?
BOY: No.

In the meantime the mother has put both her hands to her heart.

HELLINGER: Something we can see clearly here. Your mother was not available for you. She was too strongly drawn to someone else. Therefore you can only rely on your father.

Hellinger takes the boy closer to his father. The boy stands to the right of his father. The father now puts his right arm around his son and his left hand on his shoulder. The boy looks to the floor and has his hands deep in his pockets. They remain like this for a long time. For a little while the boy lifts his head very slightly, but he lets it sink down again very quickly, looking at the floor again.

HELLINGER *after a while to the boy*: Are you also looking at a dead person? A friend perhaps?
BOY: At a friend.

After a while Hellinger chooses a representative for this friend and gets him to lie in front of the boy, with his back on the floor. The other dead person turns to the side. The mother has moved even further back.

HELLINGER *to the boy*: Go to him.

The boy goes to the dead man and cries.

HELLINGER *to the boy*: Go with your movement.

After a while to this dead man: What goes on inside you?

DEAD MAN: I feel the same as him. I also look at a dead man.

The boy and the dead man look at each other. Then Hellinger puts the boy's hand on the dead man's stomach.

HELLINGER *after a while to the boy*: What goes on inside you?
BOY: I am sad.
HELLINGER: Tell him, "I think of you with love."
BOY: I think of you with love.

After a while Hellinger gets the boy to stand again and to turn to his father.

HELLINGER: Look at your father and say to him: "I am your son."
BOY: I am your son.
HELLINGER: "Look at me as your son."
BOY: Look at me as your son.
HELLINGER: "Take me as your son."
BOY: Take me as your son.
HELLINGER: "Please."
BOY: Please.

The father puts his arm around him. The boy has his hands in his pockets. Hellinger helps him put his arms around the father. Father and son remain this way for a long time. The father kisses him and strokes his head. The whole time the boy has his head turned away from the father. Again, the father strokes the boy's head and back. After a while they release each other.

HELLINGER *to the boy*: How are you now?

BOY: Good.

HELLINGER: I leave it here. All the best to you.

Example: Love

HELLINGER *to a young man about 18 years old who also lives in the street*: What is it about with you?

YOUNG MAN: I am very aggressive, and often I feel very alone.

HELLINGER: When you are aggressive, what do you do?

YOUNG MAN: I am doing something I am not conscious of. I can't control myself then.

HELLINGER: Who else in your family was also aggressive?

YOUNG MAN: In my father's family and also in my mother's family.

HELLINGER: What happened there?

YOUNG MAN: On my father's side, his father was very aggressive. He had also another wife. In my mother's family is an uncle whose son killed himself. This uncle killed his sister's boyfriend.

HELLINGER: When someone is as aggressive as you feel, then he is identified with someone in his family. You are probably identified with this uncle who killed his sister's boyfriend. Therefore we will have a look at that. Perhaps we find a way that allows you to release yourself from this. Okay?

YOUNG MAN: Yes.

Hellinger chooses a representative for the uncle who killed his sister's boyfriend, and for the uncle's son who killed himself. Then he chooses a representative for the uncle's sister and a representative for the sister's boyfriend who was killed.

Hellinger places the murdered boyfriend opposite the uncle, and the sister next to her boyfriend. He places the uncle's son farther back, sideways behind the uncle's sister.

The murdered man falls immediately to the floor, backwards. He lies on his back with his arms spread out. Then, with a loud bang, the uncle also falls backwards, flat on the floor, arms and legs splayed out.

As the young man witnesses this, he begins to sob. Hellinger puts his arm around him, and the young man puts his head on Hellinger's chest, with laboring breath. The uncle's sister remains standing motionless, next to her boyfriend on the floor.

The young man sobs loudly on Hellinger's chest.

HELLINGER *to the group*: Who is guilty here?
He points his finger to the uncle's sister. The uncle's sister is the guilty one.

She remains standing, unmoved.

HELLINGER: Who paid for this guilt?
He points to the uncle's son who killed himself. He paid for it.

The young man keeps on sobbing, with closed eyes.

HELLINGER *to the young man*: Now go to the murdered boyfriend, of your uncle's sister, and embrace him.

Hellinger takes him to the murdered man on the floor and gets him to kneel by his side. The young man looks at the murdered man and sobs loudly. But he does not have the courage to touch him. The uncle's sister still stands unmoved.

HELLINGER *to the young man*: Say to him, "I give you a place in my heart."

YOUNG MAN *sobbing loudly*: I give you a place in my heart.

HELLINGER *after a while*: Touch him. It is okay like this. Touch him.

He touches the dead man very carefully and puts one hand on his chest. The uncle's sister has turned her head around and looks down to the two men. The young man is calming down. His sobbing quiets.

    Hellinger gets him to stand again and takes him to his uncle, the murderer. There he begins to sob again. Hellinger asks him to kneel by his uncle's side. He kneels down and sobs loudly.

HELLINGER *after a while*: Touch him, too.

He carefully puts one hand on this chest and sobs loudly.

HELLINGER *after a while*: Look at him and say, "I give you a place in my heart."

YOUNG MAN *sobbing loudly*: I give you a place in my heart.

He keeps on sobbing loudly. After a while Hellinger asks him to get up. Then Hellinger takes the uncle's sister to her murdered boyfriend.

HELLINGER *to the uncle's sister*: Look at him.

The young man stands next to Hellinger, leaning on him. Hellinger puts an arm around the young man who is still sobbing loudly.

HELLINGER *to the uncle's sister*: Go down to your boyfriend.

She kneels by his side, puts one hand on his chest, bends down to him, embraces him and sobs. She strokes his face. He closes his eyes.

HELLINGER *to the group*: He closed his eyes. Only now does he have his peace.

Hellinger takes the young man to his uncle's son who killed himself. He stands in front of him and looks down to him.

HELLINGER: Tell him, "I give you a place in my heart."
YOUNG MAN *sobbing loudly*: I give you a place in my heart.
HELLINGER: Go down to him.

He goes down to him and sobs loudly.

HELLINGER: Touch him.

He puts one hand on the chest and calms down. But the dead son looks over to his father.
    Hellinger tells the uncle to get up and takes him to his son.

HELLINGER *to the uncle*: Go down to him.

The uncle kneels by his son's side. The son stretches his hand out to his father. His father takes the hand. Then the son closes his eyes.

HELLINGER *to the group*: Now his son has also closed his eyes. He atoned for his father. He paid for it.

The uncle lies down next to his son and also closes his eyes.

Hellinger asks the young man to get up and turn around to the group.

HELLINGER: Now look ahead. Look into the world. Say to all here: "Now I stand here, in the service of peace."
YOUNG MAN *breathing deeply*: Now I stand here, in the service of peace.
HELLINGER: Look at them all. Tell them: "Now I am in the service of love and peace."
YOUNG MAN: Now I am in the service of love and peace.

He breathes deeply. Hellinger takes him by the hand.

HELLINGER: Now you have really soft hands.

He is still breathing deeply.

HELLINGER: No one needs to be afraid of you any more.
YOUNG MAN: Yes.
HELLINGER: Okay. All the best to you.
YOUNG MAN: Thank you.

They embrace and shake hands.

School

From workshops for systemic pedagogy
in Mexico

Systemic pedagogy

HELLINGER: I would like to say something about systemic pedagogy. What does it mean, systemic pedagogy? It means, we do not only see the child, but we also see the parents in the child. A teacher said to me once when she stands in front of a class of twenty children, she does not only see twenty, but sixty people at once, this means their parents as well. When teachers see the parents behind the children, they understand the children. At the same time the teachers can also feel their own parents and ancestors behind them.

Well, in the Western societies one has an idea of perfect parents. I don't know what to do with that. My parents were not ideal, but very good. I am of the opinion - and this is a revolutionary sentence: All children are good, and so are all parents.

Respect for the parents as they are

This respect for the parents, for our own and those of the students with whom we are dealing, is the foundation of a good education. I have condensed this to something small. I wrote a letter to my mother – she died a long time ago, but still I wrote it.

"Dear Mama,
You are a normal person, like millions of other women. As a normal woman you conceived me and carried me in your womb. Then you gave birth to me, you fed me, you cared for me and watched over me, as a normal woman. As a normal woman you were the best mother for me that I could have. And like this, I love you, as a normal woman. I release you from those expectations of mine, which went beyond what I may expect of a normal woman. What you have given to me went far beyond what I could expect as a normal child."

144

When we look at our parents, all parents, also the parents of our students, they have done everything right. In passing life on they have done everything right. In this regard all parents are perfect. When I have them in my heart, anyone can tell me whatever they want about their parents: I respect them.

The spiritual field

Well it is a fact that every human being is embedded in a system. Not only their parents belong to this system, but also the grandparents and the ancestors. In this system a lot has happened, good things and bad. The past still has an effect in its presence.

This is a field in which all of our ancestors are present, and everything that happened as well. In this field everything is in resonance with everything else. We are all influenced by it.

What is the result? Nobody can be different from what they are. Our parents could not be different from what they were. We cannot be other than what we are. And our students cannot be different from what they are.

When we look at the students who cause problems at school, we know: they can't be other than what they are. When we look at their parents and the system from which they come, we understand why they are the way they are.

Resonance with the excluded

One thing you must keep in mind above all. A system is disturbed when someone is excluded, even if this happened many generations ago. Where a child happens to behave differently from how we would like him to behave, then this child looks at a person in the system who was excluded. Then such a child behaves differently out of a special love. Then if we would have something to do with this child, we can stand next to him and look with him at this excluded person. Perhaps we can speak with the parents about this and perhaps we can find out who this person is. If we look at this person and give the person respect, together with the parents, this person is once again included. Then the child can change. But not just the child, the family as a whole will change. Therefore when a teacher knows about these connections and has the opportunity to do this, it will have an effect in the family. Therefore the systemic pedagogy can have an effect beyond mere teaching, into the family and the society.

For some teachers who only look at their students, it is a depressing matter when they feel they can't make any progress. They experience burnout. There are simple remedies against such a burnout. We look with love beyond the children, to their parents, and we give them a place in our heart. Suddenly we are no longer alone with the problems. What we have taken upon our shoulders, as if we alone were responsible for the child, we can share with the parents, and face our work more confidently.

I will show you in practical examples how we work with difficult children, and we will see which solutions come up. Our idea was that teachers will present a case where they have difficulties with a child and together with them I will have a look for a possible solution.

"Dear Mummy"

HELLINGER *to a teacher*: What is your case?

TEACHER: It is a student from the first semester. He is a very poor student. Recently he behaved so provocatively that the teacher slapped him.

Another thing that stands out is that it is very hard for him to speak in front of several people. He speaks only very softly. At school he has the nickname, "the mute one."

HELLINGER: How old is he?

TEACHER: 15.

HELLINGER: Well let's have a look at what we can do.

Hellinger chooses a representative for the boy and places him. The representative looks instantly to the floor.

HELLINGER *to the teacher*: Do you know anything about his mother?

TEACHER: Very little.

HELLINGER: The boy looks to the floor. When someone looks to the floor, it means he or she looks to a dead person.

Hellinger chooses a woman as a representative for a dead person and gets her to lie on her back in front of the boy's representative. This woman looks up to the boy. The boy is very moved and slowly kneels by her side. After a while he sits on his heels and deeply bends down to her. The woman holds him by his arm and strokes him. He straightens up and reaches his hand out to her. Then he puts her hand in front of his eyes.

Hellinger places a female representative behind him. This representative slowly turns away from the two.

HELLINGER *to the group*: This dead woman looks past the boy.

The other woman is quite restless, with fast movements in her upper body, rocking back and forth.

Hellinger takes the boy's representative and leads him away, but to a place where the boy can see both women.

147

HELLINGER *to the boy's representative*: How is this now, better or worse?

BOY'S REPRESENTATIVE: Better.

HELLINGER *to the group*: The problem is between the two women. It has nothing to do with him.

The other woman has turned around to the dead woman who looks at her the whole time and reaches out her hand to her. The woman is twisting and turning and goes to the floor, sobbing. Very slowly, she slides over to the dead woman, touches her hand, lies flat on the floor and then on her belly. The dead woman puts her arms around the other one. They embrace tenderly.

HELLINGER *to the group*: The image is, the other woman is his mother, the dead one is her mother.

Probably his mother lost her mother early. She does not dare go to her. Now the boy can say something that he could not say until now.

To the boy: Say to your mother, "Dear Mummy."

BOY'S REPRESENTATIVE: Dear Mummy.

Hellinger leads the boy closer to the two women. His mother's representative lifts her head and looks at him.

HELLINGER *to the boy*: "Dear Mummy."

The mother's representative straightens up further. She bids her mother farewell, gets up and takes her son into her arms. They remain like this for a long time. The dead woman on the floor lies on her back and closes her eyes.

HELLINGER *to the group*: The dead woman has closed her eyes and is at peace. She is acknowledged and loved. Now she can close her eyes.

To the representatives: Thank you all.

To the teacher: How are you?

TEACHER: Good.

HELLINGER: Now you can understand the student. It is good if you visit the mother and tell her what went on here. The student should not be present. Only talk with the mother.

TEACHER: The mother is here in the group.

HELLINGER: Wonderful.

To the teacher: That's it then.

Who belongs to the family system?

HELLINGER: I would like to say something about systems, about our system. When we work systemically and speak of a system, we refer to those people who have an influence on the present, whose fates can play a role in our lives now. Therefore everyone who is related to us is also a part of our system. We must be very clear here, therefore I will list them now.

On the lowest level, the children belong to the system, all the children, including the still-born ones. In contrast to what I wrote in my earlier books, the aborted children also belong. So, all children are included.

On the next level up, the parents and their siblings belong. So besides the parents, the uncles and aunts belong, but not the partners of the uncles and aunts. And also not the cousins. Only the parents and their siblings. On the next level up, there are the grandparents, but without their siblings. Only the grandparents. Sometimes there are exceptions, when the siblings of the grandparents are also included, if they had a hard fate. But normally only the grandparents.

Occasionally also some of the great-grandparents, but only rarely so. These are the blood relatives.

But there are also other people who belong to the system without being blood relatives. As non-relatives, the partners of the parents and grandparents belong, including former partners. All those belong who made room for the members of the system. So if the father or the mother had been married before, and these partners died, or one of our parents separated from them, then we have our parents or grandparents *because* the former partners made room for them. They also belong to the system.

Entanglements

How can I say that? It turns out that the children from a second marriage imitate the former partners. They are entangled with them. There is a father for instance, who loves his daughter very much, and yet the daughter is constantly angry with him. He asks himself: "What did I do wrong?"

What did he do wrong? He separated from the first wife. Not that this is always wrong, but the daughter represents the former wife in her feelings. This woman is excluded. Perhaps they even speak badly about her.

In a system nobody can be excluded. Those who are excluded are represented. What would be the solution here? The father respects his first wife. He says to her, for instance: "I loved you very much. I am sorry we separated, whatever the reasons were." Then he can say to her, "Please look kindly at my second wife and my children." When the former partner is honored, she can be friendly. When she is included in the system, then the daughter does not have to represent her any more. With this example I have also explained what an entanglement is. Someone from a later generation must represent someone from a former generation, because this person was excluded, or perhaps forgotten. Those who represent them become difficult pupils. So we must put the system into order.

Where does the order begin? In our own soul. This means, the teachers take the whole system of the student into their hearts.

There are people who complain, for instance. There are even students who complain about their parents. Or the parents complain about their own parents or get upset with them. It is precisely those who are rejected that the teachers take into their own hearts. The teachers return the system to order in their own soul. Then they can help others.

Who belongs to the family system? (continued)

I repeat once more: Those belonging to the system are the children, the parents and their siblings, the grandparents, sometimes some of the great-grandparents and former partners of parents and grandparents. But there are still more people who belong, all those who suffered loss through our gain. I have seen this in rich families, who had been drilling for oil, or building railway lines, and workers lost their lives. Their wealth was built on the death of others. Then these people who were "lost" belong. This shows up, for instance, in the fact that later on an heir of such an enterprise will let the enterprise go down hill. Such an heir is identified with these dead people. Or families who had slaves will later on have family members who behave like slaves. They are identified with the slaves and feel like one of them.

Exercise: Dissonance and resonance

Now I will do a little exercise with you. Just close your eyes. You go into your body and you sense what in your body may be hurting.

Which organ feels unwell? Which muscle perhaps? Which bone? This organ is in dissonance with your body. But, this is my experience, this organ is perhaps looking at a person who was excluded from our family. This organ is in resonance with an excluded person. Through the pain it brings the presence of this excluded person to our attention.

Then we go into this organ and together with it, we go to this excluded person. We say to this person: "Now I see you. Now I love you. Now I take you into my heart."

If we take this person into our heart this way, the illness can ease. We regain health through bringing the excluded back into our family.

I'll take this still a bit further. Imagine you go into a large hall, like a cathedral. There are statues of all the members of your system. Some are standing in the foreground, others are still in the background, where it is dark. We go to each person, to each statue. Suddenly the statue comes to life for us. We look into the eyes of this person, we bow and we say to the person: "Thank you."

Then we go to the statues who stand more in the dark. We wait until they come to life again. Then we bow and say: "Now I see you. Now I take you also into my heart, whatever your fate was, or your guilt."

We sense what goes on inside us when we take them into our heart. We can feel how we grow, how we become complete, finally connected to all in our family.

In the same way we look at our students, especially at those who worry us. Together with them, we look at the persons whom they bring to our awareness through their behavior, and we take them into our heart. These persons help us to help these students.

Perhaps now we understand better what systemic education means. How much nicer it is than only looking at the students.

Students with learning difficulties

HELLINGER *to a teacher*: What is it about?

TEACHER: I have a student in third grade who fails in several subjects. We don't know what to do.

HELLINGER *to the group*: I have little background information. But in this work we can find out through a constellation what it is about. So I will choose a representative for the boy. Then we will have a look at what's going on.

Hellinger chooses a representative and places him.

HELLINGER *to this representative*: You collect yourself and you follow what goes on in your soul, and we observe it.

The boy's representative looks to the floor and he has his fists clenched. His head is down. He slowly turns away, sits on the floor and bows deeply.

Hellinger chooses a representative for a dead person and gets him to lie down in front of the boy's representative, with his back on the floor.

The boy's representative shakes his fists violently and thumps them on the floor.

Hellinger chooses one more representative and places him opposite the boy, with the dead person between them.

HELLINGER *to the group*: A dead person is lying on the floor. Just now he has touched the boy's head with this hand. The question is: Whom does this student represent? He represents a murderer. But it is not about this boy personally. He represents someone from the system.

In the meantime the boy has calmed down. The third representative has knelt down by the dead person and is bending down to him. He obviously represents a perpetrator.

Hellinger tells the boy's representative to get up and leads him somewhat away from the scene.

HELLINGER: How is it now?
BOY'S REPRESENTATIVE: I am relieved.

In the meantime the other representative has bent down to the dead person, nearly in the same position that the boy's representative took on before.

HELLINGER *pointing to this representative*: Here is the problem.
He points to the boy's representative: He is innocent, but identified with the murderer.

The boy's representative shrugs something off and goes further away. Then he turns away. In the meantime the other representative has laid down next to the dead person. The two hold each other by the hand.

HELLINGER *to the group*: Now the reconciliation between the murderer and his victim is beginning. They hold each other by the hand. And now the murderer weeps. Now they are reconciled.
To the boys' representative: Turn around once more. Have a look at it and bow. Then straighten up and turn away.
Afterwards: How are you now?

BOY'S REPRESENTATIVE: So much better.

HELLINGER *to the representatives*: Thank you.

After a while to the teacher: This boy is schizophrenic. Is that true?

TEACHER: Could be.

The background of schizophrenia

HELLINGER: What we have seen here is the basic dynamic behind schizophrenia. Schizophrenia is no illness. It is something systemic. Where you have someone with schizophrenia there was a murder in the family. Sometimes several generations back. These two, the victim and the perpetrator, are excluded from the system, mostly the murderer, but also the victim. The basic dynamics in a system: When someone has been excluded, this person will have to be represented by another family member. Thus, a member of the family from a later generation must represent both the victim and the perpetrator. But the two are not reconciled. The later representative senses this opposition between murderer and victim in his or her soul, and becomes confused.

What brings about healing in this situation? In such a constellation we go back to the place where the murder has occurred, and we bring the victim and the murderer together, until they are reconciled. Here we could see how this reconciliation succeeded.

When such a thing has happened, if it happened many generations ago, then in each subsequent generation there is schizophrenia. The system is schizophrenic because it carries something forward that is unreconciled. One member of the family must take on this task; often it is the family member with the greatest love. This is how the schism continues through the many generations all the way into the present. But because in such systems all members are in resonance with all others, we can go back many generations to bring something back to order, like we

155

did here. Then it is the reconciliation and healing that ripples through the generations all the way to the present time.

To the teacher: This boy is free now. Now the boy is in a better position. The family will also feel better. The question is: What will you do now? You go to the parents and tell them what went on here. The boy can be there, too. You tell them what went on, and then you leave. Then we wait for the good effect to take place in the family.

Recently I had a similar constellation in Germany. A teacher talked about a student who was so aggressive that removing him from the school seemed like the only answer. We set it up. The same evening at home, the boy was changed. For three months, he was completely changed. Then there was a relapse. For it matters that everyone in the family looks at the system, and that they take everyone into their heart. Not only the boy, but also his father must do this.

To the teacher: So sometimes some extra work is required. Okay? All the best to you and the student.

Female student with anorexia

HELLINGER *to a teacher*: What is it about?

TEACHER: About a female student in the first year of the secondary section.

HELLINGER: How old?

TEACHER: 12 years. She is in the room here with her parents. She has always been quite ill.

HELLINGER: What is her illness?

TEACHER: She suffers from depression and eating disorders.

HELLINGER: What do you mean by eating disorders?

TEACHER: It is anorexia.

HELLINGER: That will do.

Hellinger chooses a representative for the student and a representative for her father and her mother. Then he asks the teacher to place them in relationship to each other.

She places the father in such a way that he looks past his wife, into the distance. The woman stands in front of him, slightly to the left, and she looks past him as well. The daughter stands behind the father somewhat to the right, facing him.

HELLINGER *to the group*: When we look at that, we see clearly what the dynamics are in the family. It is quite clear.

He leads the father into the direction in which he had been looking, away from the family.

HELLINGER *to the father*: How is it here for you, better or worse?
FATHER'S REPRESENTATIVE: The same.
HELLINGER *to the father*: You are not collected enough. I must exchange you.

Hellinger exchanges him for another representative.

HELLINGER *to the group*: Why did I exchange him? When he came out, he had his hands clasped, first in front of his abdomen, and afterwards behind his back. I asked Angelica: "Is he experienced?" She said: "Yes." But I had my doubts. When someone says: "My feeling is the same," he is not in touch. It cannot be the same. To help the girl, I had to exchange him.

Hellinger now leads the other representative of the father out of the family.

HELLINGER *to this representative*: How are you feeling here, better or worse?

FATHER'S REPRESENTATIVE: Worse.

HELLINGER: How is the mother when the husband has gone?

MOTHER'S REPRESENTATIVE: I don't want to look at him directly, but I want to feel him by my side.

Hellinger takes the daughter behind the father.

HELLINGER *to the daughter*: How do you feel here, better or worse?

DAUGHTER'S REPRESENTATIVE: Here I see him.

HELLINGER: Do you feel better or worse?

DAUGHTER'S REPRESENTATIVE: Better.

HELLINGER *to the group*: What is the dynamic here?

When we are dealing with anorexia, it is always the same. The father wants to leave his family. We could see that in the constellation. The father looked to the outside. And the daughter? She says to him: "Rather me than you." The father does not just want to leave, he also wants to die. And the child says: "I'll die in your place." These are the dynamics that present themselves here.

Who is the client? With whom do I have to work? With the father.

To the teacher: Do you know anything about the father's family?

TEACHER: The grandfather died. The student's father has diabetes.

HELLINGER: How old was the father when his father died?

TEACHER: I don't know.

HELLINGER *to the group*: Diabetes is a severe illness. The daughter is afraid that the father might die. Then she says: "Rather me than you."

The question is: What would be the solution?

158

Hellinger goes to the father's representative and turns him towards his daughter.

HELLINGER *to the father:* You look at your daughter and you say to her: "I will stay as long as I am allowed to."
FATHER'S REPRESENTATIVE: "I will stay for as long as I'm allowed to."

Father and daughter look at each other for a long time. The daughter is very moved.

HELLINGER *after a while to the group:* Can you see the daughter's love? And her fear?
To the father's representative: Now you look at your wife and you say: "I will stay for as long as I am allowed to."
FATHER'S REPRESENTATIVE: "I will stay for as long as I am allowed to."

The mother reaches out for her husband's and her daughter's hand. She puts her head on his chest. The three embrace tenderly.

HELLINGER *after a while:* Okay, thank you.
To the teacher: Do you understand the student better?
TEACHER: Yes.
HELLINGER: Good that she is here and that she could see this.
   Okay, then all the best to you.
TEACHER: Thank you.

Children do everything
to save their parents

HELLINGER: I would like to say something about these dynamics. This brings something else to light. It brings to light why students are difficult sometimes.

Here we had no entanglement, like in the other cases. Here some basic dynamics in the family show up. Children do everything to save their parents. The love of a child is so great that the child is even willing to die for them. Children have the idea that it would help the parents if they die. Therefore it's important that teachers are aware of this.

There is an ancient and widespread idea - which is based on magical thinking - that we can wrestle a blessing from Fate or from God, if we are willing to make a sacrifice.

I recently heard a story about an Italian family. The grandfather was on a ship near Naples, as a storm broke loose. Then he promised God: If I will be saved, I will give God a child. This is quite common still. One can see it in many families. For instance when they expect a child to become a monk or a nun, so that the family is safe. The idea is that if we sacrifice something to God, then God is obliged to help us. This is a widespread fantasy. In this family the grandfather's son refused to become a priest, but the grandchild became one. Or he was prepared to become one, but then shortly before the consecration he said to his father: "If I must become a priest, I will kill myself." That brought his father to his senses, and the father said to his son: "As far as I'm concerned, you are free to live."

This has something to do with the dynamics in our own soul and in relationships. Let's take husband and wife, for instance. The man gives something to his wife, and the wife is happy about it. But she feels guilty now. She thinks: "Now I must give him something, too." So she gives him something, but because she loves him, she gives him a little bit more. Then he feels guilty. So he gives her something, and a little bit more, out of love.

So, we have a need for balance. When we give something we expect something in return. This is good for human relationships, but now we transfer this experience to Fate and to God. We think, if we make a promise to Fate, then it must help. In this case the girl says: "I'll die in your place." The girl expects that if she dies, Fate will spare her father's life. This concept is widespread, especially amongst children. We must know this. So much for the dynamic: "I in your place."

There are also other dynamics that we must be aware of, but we will talk about that later. I wanted to explain it through the example of this constellation.

Teachers and parents

First of all I want to say something general. I also was a teacher once. I led a big school in Africa. Therefore I know how teachers feel, how students feel, and how those feel who must lead a school.

Teachers come into the life of children later on. The parents were there from the start. They gave their children life. This is the greatest service that a human being can render. The teacher supports the parents in this. When teachers look at the students, they see their parents behind them. They take the students' parents into their hearts, no matter what they are like. For all parents are perfect. As parents they are perfect. In passing life on they did everything right. They did not hold anything back, and they could not add anything to it either. They passed on what they received. In this regard there are only perfect parents.

Some parents have difficulties in the upbringing of their children. The reason for this is that they also come from a family in which there were difficulties. Nevertheless whenever children leave a family and start a family of their own, they come from a family who did the right thing. This family may have done things differently than another family, for all families are different. But all of them are right. Therefore teachers will honor the specialty of the student's family when they meet a child, without the idea that the child should change.

When we look at life, we see how multifaceted it is. Not only is each human different from all others, each family is different as well. But each family passes on something special to the children.

Some people have the idea that there could be an ideal family, and other families should follow this model. But in a family that we perhaps see as difficult, and where the children experience burdensome things, the difficult and burdensome issues give the children a special strength which children from ideal families do not have. Therefore the basic attitude that serves life best is agreeing to everything as it is, without the wish to change anything.

When I meet people with this attitude of agreeing, they need not be afraid of me, for instance, that I might want to change something in their family or that I am critical of them. Instead, they can meet me as an equal. Then new possibilities develop between us.

Now I would like to show you an example of how one can relate to a family who says they have difficulties with a child. Afterwards I will say more about it.

Mummy, I will die in your place

Hellinger asks a boy's parents to sit next to him. The parents say that their son does not want to learn anything at school.

HELLINGER *to the group*: I spoke with these parents earlier. They told me they are divorced. Over there is their son. They say that they have problems with him. But children are never difficult. Do you know that? There are no difficult children. What appears to be difficult, is in fact a special love in the child. The child who causes problems is connected to someone who has no place in the family. Therefore I do not look at the child. I let him sit where he sits. First I want to speak with his parents, to find out whom the child loves, deep inside and secretly. Then the parents can also look at the child differently, and this boy here can see himself differently too.

The parents nod.

HELLINGER *to the parents*: I liked him instantly.

The parents beam. The father looks over to the son, and taps his chest.

HELLINGER: I also liked the father. And the mother? She has difficulties. What they are we don't know.
To the group: I will demonstrate how we can proceed here.

Hellinger chooses a representative for the mother and sets her up.

HELLINGER *to this representative*: You represent the mother. Allow to happen whatever goes on in your body. We will just observe.

163

The mother's representative breathes heavily. She puts her hand to her chest and begins to shake, while she is also looking to the floor.

Hellinger chooses a further representative and asks her to lie in front of the mother's representative, with her back on the floor. The mother's representative clenches her fists.

HELLINGER *to the group*: Look at her hands.

The mother's representative presses her hands to her chest as if in great pain.

Hellinger now calls the boy and asks him to lie next to the person on the floor. The mother's representative moves backwards several steps. She releases her fists, but keeps pressing her chest, as if in great pain, whilst also breathing heavily and hunching over.

HELLINGER *to the mother's representative*: Do you feel better or worse since your son is lying there?

THE MOTHER'S REPRESENTATIVE *can hardly speak*: I am in pain.
HELLINGER *as the mother wants to say something*: Don't speak. Go closer.

Bent over in great pain she moves closer to the woman on the floor.

HELLINGER: Look at it.

The mother's representative cringes in great pain and goes back again. Then she straightens up a bit.

HELLINGER *to the son on the floor*: How do you feel here?
SON: I am fine here.

The mother's representative is still pressing her hands on her chest in great pain.

Hellinger now asks the son to get up and stand opposite his mother, with the woman on the floor between them. This woman looks across to the mother. The mother's representative calms down and straightens up.

HELLINGER *to the group*: The woman on the floor is a dead person. She looks across to the mother's representative. She wants something from her. But we don't know who she is.

After a while Hellinger gets the mother to take the place of her representative. She remains standing there without moving for a long time. Then she gesticulates helplessly.

HELLINGER *after a while to the mother*: This dead person is yours. She is a dead child.
MOTHER: It is my oldest son, who is far away from me.
HELLINGER *to the group*: If there's talking, it usually takes away energy. We can see everything in the movements of the representatives. From everything we could see here, my image is, the dead person is an aborted child.

The mother nods.

HELLINGER: Yes, look at it.

The mother breathes deeply and begins to sob.

HELLINGER *to the group*: Her son loves this child and wants it to be remembered.

The father is also affected and nods; he also breathes deeply.

HELLINGER *to the group*: I will not go any further here; I only brought it to light. Now we can understand better what is going on in the child.

Now I will briefly explain the dynamics. The mother wants to die. She wants to follow the child. Her son says to her: "Dear Mummy, I will die in your place." Therefore, he does not need to do anything at school, what for? If he wants to die, he doesn't need to do anything.

Now Hellinger places the father opposite the son.

HELLINGER *to the father*: Wait a little. Go into your feelings first and look at your son.

Father and son look at each other. The father smiles at him. Hellinger nudges the son a bit closer to the father. The father goes towards him, and they embrace for a long time. Then Hellinger gets the son to turn around and leads him a few steps forward.

HELLINGER *to the son*: How do you feel here, better or worse?
SON: Worse.

Hellinger tells the father to sit down again.

HELLINGER *to the group*: The son feels better now. We could see that: He feels better there than with his father. The father does not give him enough support. I will interrupt it here. Thanks to the representatives.

The parents and the boy sit down next to Hellinger.

166

Helping in accord with the child's fate

HELLINGER *to the group*: As teachers you are sometimes confronted with such situations. There is a difficult child. The child does not achieve anything any more at school, and you think perhaps you get some help from the parents. But sometimes you don't get any help from the parents, like here. The question is: What can we do then? I see in your faces that this is a difficult question, because you are so often confronted with such a situation.

To the directors of this school: Now I will do an exercise with you.

Hellinger places the two directors of the school side by side, and the boy opposite them. Far behind this boy he places a representative for the boy's fate.

HELLINGER *to the directors of this school*: Instead of looking at the boy, look at his fate.

After a while the female director bows to the boy's fate and looks up again.

HELLINGER *to the directors of the school*: How are you now?

FIRST DIRECTOR: Better.

SECOND DIRECTOR: Better.

HELLINGER *to the group*: When we look at the boy, how is he feeling now? He is better.

To the representatives: Thank you.

To the group: As helpers we often have the idea that we must keep people alive at any cost and help them to a happy life. But we are all exposed to other powers, and our efforts may be to no avail. Instead of just seeing one person standing opposite us who is seeking or needing our help, we look beyond them. Suddenly we sense there are other powers at work, far greater than us. Then we calm down. Often we can also look at the child differently, without concern.

As the directors smile and nod: This is the relief. Now I did something especially for the teachers.

Without concern

HELLINGER *to the group*: When something happens like this situation here, where both parents are entangled and still remain entangled for some time, we need not worry.

To the parents: I am not concerned about the mother, and I am not concerned about the father. Something came to light that set something in motion in our soul.

It had an effect, especially for the mother. This movement continues on, and it takes its time. Then some weeks or months later you are perhaps surprised that something is different. Keep on being surprised! Okay? All the best to you.

Both parents thank Hellinger.

HELLINGER *to the father*: Your son needs his father. Give him a place in your heart.

Piercing

HELLINGER *to the group*: There are signals of which we must take notice, also in our students. Those who get some piercing done on themselves have abandoned respect for their lives. This boy here is one of them.

Would you do this to a human being that you love? Would you do that? They do it to their own body! They have renounced their lives. This is a signal, and we must take it seriously.

Luckily, of course, one can remove such a thing again.

To this boy: Okay?

He nods.

Difficult children

HELLINGER *to the group*: I would like to say something about illnesses. Perhaps you think this has nothing to do with what is going on here. But I have seen that when someone has a particular illness, especially a life-threatening illness, or a special physical complaint, then what hurts or makes one ill is in resonance with another person who was forgotten or excluded from the family. So, even though the illness turns away from us, it turns to another person and wants to direct our attention to this person. When we honor this person, when we take this person into our heart, the illness can go. Often it can simply go then. It has served its purpose.

It is the same with a difficult child. The difficult child is in resonance with another person, like for instance this boy here. He was in resonance with the aborted child. Then we may want to alleviate the difficulty, for instance through wise admonishing, which is futile as we know. It will be better to look together with the child at the person in the family who wants to be brought back in. The mere thought of it already relieves the child. The child no longer feels "treated" by us, as we walk a certain path together. Then the child can feel safe with us.

The hidden love

HELLINGER *to a boy who's about 16 years old*: I have heard that you are a bit lively at school. Is that so?

BOY: Yes.

HELLINGER: What are you doing when you are so lively?

BOY: I play up a bit in class sometimes.

HELLINGER: What are you doing when you play up like this?

BOY: I become explosive.

HELLINGER: You have quite a bit of energy.

BOY: Yes.

HELLINGER: When one can't do anything useful with this energy, one has to do something like that.

BOY: Yes.

HELLINGER: Who else in your family is so energetic?

BOY: Nobody.

HELLINGER: Are you the only one?

BOY: Yes.

HELLINGER: Are your parents still together?

BOY: No.

HELLINGER: What happened?

BOY: They separated ten years ago.

HELLINGER: With whom are you now?

BOY: With my dad.

HELLINGER: You like him a lot.

BOY: Yes.

The boy is very moved and nods.

HELLINGER: I can see that.

The boy is happy and nods.

HELLINGER: How is your dad doing?

BOY: Badly.

HELLINGER: What is the matter with him?

BOY: His health is very bad.

HELLINGER: What problems has he got?

BOY *sighs*: He has a lung edema and insufficiency of the kidneys. I don't know what else he has got.

HELLINGER: Okay, I will work with you and your father. Yes?

BOY: Yes.

Hellinger chooses a representative for the father and sets him up.

HELLINGER *to this representative*: Now you take the father of this boy into your heart. You take note of what goes on in your body, and you follow that. Then we look for a good solution for all.

The father's representative remains standing for a long time without moving.

HELLINGER *to the boy*: Did something special happen in your father's family?

BOY: Like what for instance?

HELLINGER: Did someone die young?

BOY: Yes.

HELLINGER: Who?

BOY: His father.

HELLINGER: How old was your father when his father died?

BOY: 19 years.

HELLINGER: What did his father die from?

BOY: I personally don't know.

HELLINGER: Is someone from your family here?

BOY: Yes, my mother.

Hellinger calls out for the mother to come over and gets her to sit next to him.

HELLINGER: *to the mother*: What happened in the family of his father?
MOTHER: His father's father died at age 45 during an operation for a stomach ulcer.

Hellinger chooses a representative and asks him to lie down in front of the father, with his back on the floor.

HELLINGER *to the group*: The representative's glance went to the floor. Therefore I put someone on the floor in front of him. I don't know who it is, but perhaps it is his father.

After a while Hellinger places the boy opposite his father, but with the dead man between them.

HELLINGER *to the boy*: Say to your father: "Please stay."
BOY: Please stay.
HELLINGER *after a while*: Say it once more.
BOY: Please stay.

He says it in an aggressive voice and with his fists clenched.

HELLINGER *after a while*: Shout it out very loudly.
BOY: Please stay!

He shouts it with deep emotion and cries. Hellinger tells him several times to repeat it very loudly. Then the boy begins to sob.

Hellinger takes him to stand in front of his father.

HELLINGER *to the boy as he stands in front of his father*: Say:
"Please stay."
BOY: Please stay.
HELLINGER: "Please."
BOY: Please stay.
HELLINGER: "Please."
BOY: Please stay.
HELLINGER: "Please."
BOY: Please stay.
HELLINGER: "Please."
BOY: Please.

He still has his fists clenched. The father doesn't move.

HELLINGER *to the father*: Tell him: "I am dying."
FATHER: I am dying.
HELLINGER *to the boy*: Say: "Please stay."
BOY: Please stay.
HELLINGER *to the father*: Say: "I am dying."
FATHER: I am dying.
HELLINGER: "I am ill. I am dying."
FATHER: I am ill. I am dying.
HELLINGER: "Like my father."
FATHER: I am ill. I am dying.
HELLINGER: "Like my father."
FATHER *with a clear voice*: Like my father.

*Father and son look at each other for a long time. The boy breathes
deeply, still with clenched fists. Then he lowers his head and eases
his fists.*

HELLINGER *to the boy*: Say: "Dear Daddy."

BOY: Dear Daddy.

HELLINGER: Look at him and say: "Please stay."

BOY: Please stay.

HELLINGER *to the father*: Tell him: "Even if I die, you will always remain my son."

FATHER: Even if I die, you will always remain my son.

Hellinger takes the son closer to his father. They embrace deeply and for a long time. The father holds his son tightly and strokes his back. When they release each other, his father puts his hand on the boy's shoulder. They look at each other for a long time. The boy breathes deeply. As the father moves back one step, Hellinger asks him to lie down next to the representative of his own father and to look at him. Then he turns the boy around so that he can look at his father and grandfather on the floor.

Father and Grandfather look at each other and hold each other by the hands.

HELLINGER *after a while to the boy*: Say to your father and your grandfather: "In me you will live on."

BOY: In me you will live on.

HELLINGER: "I will stay alive, in your memory."

BOY: I will stay alive, in your memory.

HELLINGER: "I will do something great with my life, in your memory."

BOY: I will do something great with my life, in your memory.

The boy is very moved. He breathes deeply and clenches his fists again.

HELLINGER *after a while to the boy*: Lie down next to them.

He lies down on the floor next to his father, and he looks over to him. But the father does not look at his son.

HELLINGER *to the boy*: How are you there, better or worse?
BOY: Worse.
HELLINGER *to the father*: How is it for you when your son lies next to you?
FATHER: It is uncomfortable that he lies next to me.
HELLINGER: Tell your son: "Go!"
FATHER: Go!

Hellinger indicates to the son to get up. The son gets up and turns away.

HELLINGER: How is it for you now?
BOY: I am upset.

Hellinger turns him around once more to his father and grandfather and opposite them on their other side, he places a representative for death.

HELLINGER *to the boy*: This is death.

The boy clenches his fists, but death remains unmoved. The boy breathes deeply and looks again at his father on the floor. He breathes faster and faster, obviously full of rage.

HELLINGER *after a while to the boy*: Tell death: "I will conquer you!"
BOY *with an aggressive voice*: I will conquer you!

HELLINGER: Shout it out loud.

BOY *shouting out loud and aggressively*: I will conquer you!

He looks at death for a long time, full of aggression.

HELLINGER: "I will conquer you."

BOY: I will conquer you.

HELLINGER: "Even if it costs me my life."

BOY *in a challenging and aggressive voice*: Even if it costs me my life.

He still has his fists clenched. Death remains unmoved and looks at the dead.

HELLINGER *to the boy*: Death does not look at you. You're nonexistent for him.

The boy looks again at his father and grandfather on the floor. After a while he breathes deeply and begins to cry. His whole body is shaking with sobbing. In between he looks over to death and droops his head. He wipes the tears from his face. He struggles with his turmoil for a long time, and eventually he releases his fists.

HELLINGER *to the boy*: Tell your father and grandfather: "I will stay here a little longer."

BOY: I will stay here a little longer.

HELLINGER: "Then I will die too."

BOY: Then I will die too.

HELLINGER *to the group*: Now he releases his hands. Now the aggression is gone.

To the boy: Now you are with the truth. Now you are big. Only children are furious. Okay?

BOY: Yes.

HELLINGER *to the representatives*: Thank you all.

The boy sits down next to Hellinger again.

HELLINGER *to the mother*: How are you?

MOTHER *sighs*: Better.

HELLINGER: Don't you have a great son?

MOTHER: Yes, a great son.

HELLINGER: He's got so much love.

The son breathes deeply.

MOTHER: Yes.

HELLINGER: Exactly.

The boy looks over to Hellinger in relief. Hellinger deals him a playful blow between the shoulder blades.

HELLINGER: Now you are knighted.

The boy laughs, and the group laughs with him. Hellinger and the boy shake hands.

HELLINGER: Okay, all the best to you.

Loud clapping in the group.

HELLINGER *to the group*: What I did just now, that I hit him, is only one side. When something consequential has changed in someone's life, a physical blow is needed, even if not quite as forceful as this one was. Then the change is anchored in the nervous system.

To the teachers present: Now the teachers will be happy when he returns to his class. There are only good children. One just has to find the hiding place of their love. Here it was wonderfully revealed where his love had been hiding.

Almighty power and powerlessness

We need to take note of something important here. Many think they could take life into their hands, as if they had the power over life and death. Especially children believe this. Therefore children often have the idea in their soul that their parents would be better off, if they as the children were to take on some suffering in the parents' place, as if they had the power to redeem their parents through their sacrifice. Then in their soul they say sometimes: "It's better if I die than you." This gives them feelings of almighty power.

How do children become adults? Through knowing how limited their power is. Getting there is a hard struggle, for many adults still have the idea that they could free others from their fate. Some teachers also think they could change something about their students. Some even have the idea they could change the world. They, too, find out soon enough that it is impossible. How hard this struggle is, how hard it is to give up fantasies and to face reality instead. We could see it with this boy. What a fight he put up! But he came through successfully.

The short life

HELLINGER *to a boy, about 15 years old, who raised his hand to work*: Into what kind of trouble do you get?

BOY: What do you mean?

HELLINGER: Do you cause trouble to some people?

BOY: Yes.

HELLINGER: What kind of trouble do you cause them?

BOY: I don't get involved in school.

HELLINGER: Ah, you are lazy? I was also lazy once. But only when I was little.

They laugh at each other.

HELLINGER: You don't believe me?

BOY: No.

HELLINGER: For some it's not worth the effort to do something at school.

The boy looks at Hellinger as if waiting for the explanation.

HELLINGER: Especially those who think that they won't get old anyway.

The boy changes to a somber mood and nods.

HELLINGER: Why should they make an effort?

They look at each other. Then the boy looks to the floor, pensively.

HELLINGER: I will tell you something. In order to die, one doesn't have to go to school. Everyone can do this, without having gone to school.

The boy nods.

HELLINGER: It's a different matter with life.

They look at each other. The boy nods.

HELLINGER: Just close your eyes. Imagine you go into childhood. Then you go up the ladder of life. Each rung on this ladder is one year. You go up, all the way to the rung where you are now.
After a while: How many rungs do you still see ahead of you?

The boy gets very serious.

BOY: Ten.
HELLINGER: That's very little.

The boy shakes his head.

HELLINGER: Ten rungs isn't much. That's not worth the effort at school.

The boy has become very serious.

HELLINGER: Shall we do something, the two of us?

The boy nods.

HELLINGER: Really?

Hellinger reaches his hand out to him. The boy takes it.

HELLINGER: You agree?

The boy nods.

HELLINGER: Okay, then I will do something with you. Tell me something about your family. Are your parents together?

BOY: Yes.

HELLINGER: Do you have siblings?

BOY: Yes, an older sister.

HELLINGER: Was one of your parents in an earlier relationship?

BOY: I don't know.

The boy says that his parents are also in the room. Hellinger asks them to sit next to him.

HELLINGER *to the father*: Did anything special happen in your family of origin?

FATHER: There was a murder.

HELLINGER: Who was murdered?

FATHER: My mother's father was murdered.

HELLINGER: By whom?

FATHER: By some murderer, we don't know whom.

HELLINGER: How old was your grandfather?

FATHER: About forty.

Hellinger chooses a representative for the murdered grandfather and places him. After a while the grandfather looks around and then spins around. He looks everywhere as though looking at dead bodies all over the ground.

HELLINGER *to the father*: Was the grandfather in the war or any other conflicts?

FATHER: He was a boxer.

HELLINGER: Did anyone die in a boxing match?

FATHER: No.

HELLINGER: He looks at many dead people.

FATHER: I don't know if he killed someone.

HELLINGER: I am not saying that he killed someone. But he looks at many dead people.

FATHER: Many of his children died young. My mother is 60 now. Since she was 48, she has had many strange illnesses.

HELLINGER: I'll try out something.

Hellinger chooses six women and gets them to lie down on the floor in front of the grandfather. After a while he asks the boy to lie down with the others.

The grandfather kneels down and wants to touch the women, one after the other. But they want to move away from him.

HELLINGER *to the group*: You can see how the women are afraid of him.

On his knees, the grandfather slides toward the next woman. He wants to touch her, but hesitates.

HELLINGER *to the group*: The grandfather is afraid of touching them.

After a while to the boy: How are you doing here?

BOY: This does not concern me.

HELLINGER: Exactly. Who has finished with life, is not concerned any more.

The grandfather keeps on sliding on the floor, now reaching the sixth woman. Hellinger tells the boy to get up again and to sit next to him.

HELLINGER *to the mother*: Did something special happen in your family?
MOTHER: No.

Hellinger asks the grandfather to lie down next to the dead women.

HELLINGER *to the grandfather*: Are you feeling better here or worse?
GRANDFATHER: I am a bit calmer.
HELLINGER *to the representatives*: You can take your seats again. Thank you all.

Now Hellinger places the father and opposite him, a woman.

HELLINGER *to this woman*: You are the secret of this family.

After a while the secret turns around, turning her back to the father. The father backs away one step and then one more.

HELLINGER *to the father*: Do you know what the secret is?
FATHER: I think it is my mother.
HELLINGER: What was the matter with her?

FATHER: I think she does not want to live.
HELLINGER: Ah well.

Hellinger takes the father to stand before the secret, his mother.

HELLINGER *to the father*: Look at her and say to her: "Please stay."

The father is very moved and hesitates. Then he looks to the floor.

HELLINGER *after a while*: Say it.

FATHER: Please stay.

He and his mother look at each other a long time. After a while Hellinger leads the mother away from the action, away from her son.

HELLINGER *to the mother*: How are you doing here?
MOTHER: Better.

Hellinger gets the father and his mother's representative to sit down.

HELLINGER *to the boy*: How is it with you now?

BOY: I wonder about that, too.

HELLINGER *to the group*: We're not getting anywhere here. There is a secret.
To the boy: I have a suggestion: Behave as if you only have ten years to live.
BOY: How?
HELLINGER: How, that's up to you. Ten years. You can begin with it right now.
BOY: What do you mean?
HELLINGER Behave as if you have ten years left to live.

The boy thinks about it for a long time and gets restless.

HELLINGER *after a while to the boy*: Look at your parents and say to them: "Ten years, I will definitely still live that long!"

BOY *looking at his parents*: I will at least live for another ten years.

184

HELLINGER: "I behave as if I still had at least another ten years to live."

BOY: I behave as if I still had at least another ten years to live.

The boy and his parents look at each other for a long time. Then the boy turns his gaze away from them.

HELLINGER *to the boy*: Look at them once more and say, "You don't need to worry."

BOY: You don't need to worry.

HELLINGER: "At least for the next ten years I will still be doing something."

BOY: At least for the next ten years I will still be doing something.

HELLINGER: "Perhaps even something that you will feel good about."

The boy begins to say it and suddenly stops and laughs. His parents join in.

HELLINGER: Okay, I leave it here.

To the boy: All the best to you.

Bless me if I stay alive

HELLINGER *to the group*: I would like to add something general.

When we contemplate what we saw this morning, we see what appears to be superficially important. But behind the scene we also see something else is at work, and the individual is at the mercy of something that does not reveal itself easily. When for instance a student behaves strangely at school, some say: "Well, he could change, he would just have to have some good will." But it isn't like that. Other powers are at work, and the people involved do not understand what's really going on.

I talked with the father once more, and I also got some feedback. I looked at the whole thing once more. For instance, when we placed the grandfather, some women in the group got a fright. They felt threatened. Also from what we saw in the constellation, it became clear that something terrible must have happened.

To the father: Then I placed the secret, and you said it is your mother. It showed that your mother wants to die. Why does she want to die? She wants to go to the grandfather's dead people.

When you said: "This is my mother," you smiled. You know that something is hidden there. My assumption is that in your heart you say to your mother: "Rather me than you." Your son senses this. So he says to you, his father, with deep love: "Rather me than you."

Then I said something to the father in the break that will perhaps help the boy. The boy shall go to these dead and to your grandfather, and say to them: "Bless me if I stay alive." And he shall go to your mother and say to her inside: "Bless me if I stay alive." And inside he shall say to you, his father: "Dear Daddy, bless me if I stay alive."

To the father: You are doing this anyway; of course you're doing it.

The father is very moved and nods.

FATHER: I do it with my heart.
HELLINGER: Exactly. You do it with your heart.
FATHER: Thank you.

Entanglement

HELLINGER *to the group*: We are embedded in the fates or our family, over many generations. When we meet people who behave strangely according to our understanding, we know that they are bound up in something they don't understand. Then we look

186

beyond them, and without interfering we honor their particular fate. Through our honoring it, without wanting to do something about it, they gain strength.

We often have the concept of the free human will. We have some free will, but it is limited. Where it is about the big things, such as life and death, other powers are in charge.

What can we do then? We entrust ourselves to these powers, also concerning our fate. When we have entrusted ourselves to these powers, we sometimes help others, but in accord with these greater powers.

Then the work of the teacher is easier, the parents' work is easier, and the children can feel better. Behind all this is a mighty trust that in the end everything comes together, and the differences we create between good and bad will eventually collapse. Then we have neither good nor bad people, and instead, just human beings.

I loved your father very much

HELLINGER: Was there still someone who wanted to work with me?

A teacher calls a girl about 16 years of age, who sits down next to Hellinger, and her mother. The girl looks briefly to Hellinger, smiles, and looks to the floor.

HELLINGER *to the group*: When you look at her, how old is she in her soul and in her feeling? Three years. Something happened when she was three years old.
To the girl: What happened?
HELLINGER *to the mother*: What happened when she was three years old?
MOTHER: When she was three years old, we moved in with my present husband.

The girl begins to cry and then sobs.

HELLINGER: What about her father?

MOTHER: Her daddy left us. He went away with another woman.

HELLINGER: She misses her father, we see that immediately. She misses her father.

Hellinger looks over to her. She shakes her head vehemently.

HELLINGER *to the group*: She shakes her head. Do you know why? She is afraid to admit it in front of her mother.

Hellinger looks over to the mother.

HELLINGER *to the mother*: Tell her: "I loved your father very much."

MOTHER: I loved your father very much.

HELLINGER: Say it with love.

As she wants to answer straight away: Slowly. Remember how much you loved him. Then say it from your soul.

She sighs deeply.

HELLINGER: Look at her.

MOTHER: I loved your father very much.

The mother is deeply moved. The girl cries.

Hellinger asks the mother to sit next to her daughter and to take her into her arms. She embraces the daughter, kisses and strokes her. Then they sit hand in hand.

HELLINGER *to the group*: This is all I have to do.

To the mother: All the best to you.

Both parents

HELLINGER *to the group*: I would like to say something about this. Each child has two parents. The child always needs both parents. A child must be allowed to love both parents. A child does not understand why parents separate. A child loves them both equally. But sometimes when the parents separate and the child stays with the mother, then he or she depends on the mother in every way. Sometimes the child is afraid to show the love for the father. For there is a fear that the mother will be angry, and then the child might lose the mother also. But secretly the love for the father continues on. When the child hears from the mother that she loved the father very much, then she can show the mother that she loves the father too. Then the child feels relieved.

The mother here understood this well. Now the child can easily say that she loves her father. And she knows that she can go to him. That will make her feel good. Now she feels happy.

To the girl: It's okay. You can show it. Your mother is glad too.

Mother and daughter laugh at each other. The mother puts her arm around her and kisses her.

HELLINGER *to the group*: That was still due.

Mummy, for you I will do anything

A boy, about 14 years old, sits down next to Hellinger.

HELLINGER *to this boy*: Hello. Do you want to work with me?

BOY: Yes.

HELLINGER *to the group*: He says it with strength.

To the boy: I like that. Do you have difficulties?

BOY: Yes.

HELLINGER: What kind of?

BOY: At school and at home.

HELLINGER: What is going on at home?

BOY: I easily get angry with my father.

HELLINGER: Who else is angry about your father?

BOY: Only me.

HELLINGER: I know who else is angry. Your mother of course. Do you know how I see this? You are your mother's boy.

The boy looks over to Hellinger and ponders for a long time.

HELLINGER: What would happen if your mother said: "I honor your father." What would happen?

BOY: For me? I think I would be happy.

HELLINGER: Yes? Then we will try it out and see how it feels. Okay?

BOY: Yes.

HELLINGER *to the group*: I personally can go wrong all the time, as you know. But a constellation doesn't.

Hellinger chooses a representative; it is the boy from the constellation "The short life."

HELLINGER *to this boy*: Can I rely on you?

The boy nods.

HELLINGER: You are his father.

Then Hellinger chooses a representative for the mother. This is the girl from the previous constellation "I loved your father very much."

HELLINGER *to these representatives*: You note carefully what goes on in your body and in your soul, and you behave like that.

The mother's representative looks to the floor. She tries to turn away, but hesitates.

Hellinger asks a woman to lie in front of the mother, with her back on the floor. After a while the mother takes several steps back. The dead woman is quite restless.

Hellinger places the boy in front of his mother's representative.

HELLINGER *to the boy*: Tell your mother: "Mummy, for you I'll do anything."
BOY: Mummy, for you I'll do anything.
HELLINGER: Say it from the heart and say it slowly.
BOY: Mummy, for you I'll do anything.

They look at each other for a long time. The mother clenches her fists.

HELLINGER *to the mother*: Tell him: "I am angry."
MOTHER: I am angry.
HELLINGER *after a while to the boy*: Tell her again, "Mummy, for you I'll do anything."

BOY: Mummy, for you I'll do anything.
HELLINGER *to the mother*: Tell him: "I am angry."
MOTHER: I am angry.

Mother and son look at each other for a long time. Then Hellinger takes the boy aside, so that the mother stands directly opposite the dead woman.

HELLINGER *to the mother*: Say to the dead woman, "I am angry."
MOTHER: I am angry.
HELLINGER: "I don't want you."
MOTHER: I don't want you.
HELLINGER: "Go away!"
MOTHER: Go away!
HELLINGER: Say it in a loud voice.
MOTHER *in a loud voice*: Go away!

She is clenching her fists as she shouts. She takes a few more steps backwards. The dead woman has turned towards her.

HELLINGER *to the mother*: Say it out loud.
MOTHER: Go away!

Now Hellinger takes the boy in front of his father's representative. They look at each other for a long time.

HELLINGER *to the boy*: Say to your father: "Dear Daddy, look at me as your son."

BOY: Dear Daddy, look at me as your son.
HELLINGER: "Here you are big, and I am small."
BOY: Here you are big, and I am small.

HELLINGER: "I am just a child."

BOY: I am just a child.

HELLINGER *to the group*: If you listen you notice he talks as if he is the big one.

The boy looks at Hellinger and smiles.

HELLINGER: *Say it once more*: "Dear Daddy, please look at me as your son."

BOY: Dear Daddy, please look at me as your son.

He has said it again in an arrogant voice, and the group is laughing.

HELLINGER *to the boy*: Now get on your knees and look up to him. Say, "Dear Daddy, now I respect you as my father."

BOY: Dear Daddy, now I respect you as my father.

He has said it in an arrogant voice again. The father remains unmoved.

Hellinger now takes the mother where the dead woman can see her. The dead woman is reaching her hand out for her. Again, the mother takes a few steps backward. Hellinger takes her closer to the dead woman again.

HELLINGER *to the mother*: Tell her, "Now I look at you."

MOTHER: Now I look at you.

HELLINGER: "As my child."

MOTHER: As my child.

HELLINGER *to the mother*: Go closer.

The mother slowly goes closer, until the dead woman can reach her feet with her hands stretched out. The mother remains standing like this. Hellinger goes to the boy again.

HELLINGER *to the boy*: Say to your father: "Please look at me as your son."
BOY *again in an arrogant tone*: Please look at me as your son.
HELLINGER *to the father*: Say to him: "Not yet."
FATHER: Not yet.
HELLINGER *to the son*: Go with your movement, as you sense it.

The boy gets up.

HELLINGER *to the group*: This was not the movement. We could see what the movement is. Those who are angry with their father have lost him.
To the boy: Say it once more: "Please look at me as your son."

He says it once more in an arrogant voice.

HELLINGER *to the group*: He has lost his father, poor boy. No strength. Without father, no strength.
After a while to the boy: Now say to your father, "Save me."
BOY: Save me.
HELLINGER *to the group*: It is not possible. He has lost his father – and the mother as well.

The mother had not moved either.

HELLINGER: Here I interrupt it.
To the representatives: Thank you all.

To the representatives of the father and the mother: You two representatives were very good. I could rely on you.

To the group: The father must not do anything to make it easier for the son. After the son has despised him, the father is not allowed to do anything to make it easier for him. The father's representative showed this very well.

What are the dynamics here? The mother feels guilty about the death of a child. She does not want the child. She has the rage.

To the boy: She wants to die. And you say to her: "For you I will do anything – even dying."

After a while: Only one person can save you – your father.

But only once you respect him.

The boy is serious now.

HELLINGER: Let this work in your soul. Perhaps you will find a way. But only if you become small, small before your father. Before our parents we are always small.

To the group: Those who think they are bigger than their parents have lost them. They must put on a big show without being big.

To the boy: I think you have got it now.

All the best to you.

They shake hands.

HELLINGER *to the teachers*: Were these two representatives not great? They are still completely unspoiled. Both were very good. This shows we can also do constellations with young people, even with children. This way, often even more comes to light than when we work with adults. We can always rely on the goodness in a child's soul.

The Hellinger Pedagogy

The Hellinger Pedagogy is a systemic pedagogy. What effect does it bring to a school?

I was moved when the president and director of the CUDEC, Alfonso Malpica Cárdenas, expressed his deep gratitude to me, because the systemic perspective has essentially contributed to regaining the parents' confidence in the school.

This was my third visit to this institution. I had already been invited by CUDEC in 2001 and in 2003, to help parents, teachers, and students through family constellations. At this congress I was greeted as a special guest with standing ovations. It felt as though the applause would not end.

In a certain way this meeting was an act of acknowledgment of the systemic-phenomenological approach, for the foundation of the development of systemic pedagogy that has been practiced at CUDEC for many years. However, I emphasized that this success was only possible through the pioneering work that had been already been done by Angelica and Alfonso Malpica in earlier years.

I had worked with family constellations in the form of supervision in the presence of students and their parents, about problems such as attention deficit, hyperactivity, and dyslexia, but also psychoses and drug and alcohol consumption. Confronted with problems of this kind, teachers often feel out of their depth to impart the learning contents appropriately.

The question about culprits comes up. Whose fault is the failure of the students? The parents', the teachers', the school's? But instead of looking for culprits, I found solutions in the students' family history.

The participants could observe in an impressive way the kind of love children are entangled with in their family systems, and how a student's loyalty to a family member can influence the student's learning behavior. It became clear in the constellations that teachers lose energy when they only look at the learning problems of their students. But when they look at the students and at their parents behind them, and honor the history of the family and the conditions in which a child grows up, then the teachers can be in resonance with the child's fate and with that of the whole family.

At the same time the teachers can also feel and honor their own parents standing behind them. This way they can be connected to their own strength. This way the teachers can focus on their own task and gain the necessary trust of the parents. Only this way will it become possible for them to teach the children. They leave the children and their parents in their dignity, and they take on their appropriate place as teachers.

The right order

An essential aspect of systemic pedagogy also means that the school is run in a systemic-phenomenological way. Some directors present their problems with their staff, and I demonstrate a type of work in the circle. Here the director gives every colleague a chance to speak, so that afterwards appropriate decisions that take all the concerns into account can be made.

It has also become clear that the cohesion between teachers and the next hierarchical level, the directors, is important. A teacher who works against the director is no longer tenable for the school. The same applies when teachers join ranks with students against other teachers.

The teaching body is a system that is bound to certain orders. The first person is the director, then the teachers, who are all equal, except in the order of priority. Who came first to this school as a teacher has priority over those who came later. The newly arrived teachers often would like to show the old teachers how one should do things, and there we go, trouble is brewing. It is important to acknowledge the capacity and competence of each one, for they are all different.

When we acknowledge that everyone is good in his or her own way, and that everyone teaches in his or her own special way, then there can be harmony between all.

In order to deal with the dreaded burnout syndrome, the teachers must be allowed to take up the appropriate position of a teaching person.

In the first place are always the parents, then the students, and the teachers come last. The safest place from which teachers can teach is the lowest. There they have the most strength. Their fate and resonance are coming to their aid, and thus they receive the strength to do their work.

Once the teachers truly see themselves as the last one in the row of student-parents-teachers, only then the needed foundation for teaching is created. This way the teachers do not feel so alone, they share the burden, and so they take a step back to continue their work with joy.

Mutual respect is the foundation of a good education.

Part Two:
The Course of Love

Mystic Consciousness (I)

Workshop in Bozen, Italy, 2013

Introduction

HELLINGER: I am happy to be here, and to have such a good translator by my side.

The topic for this workshop is: Success in life - success in work. The successes in life come first, then comes the success in work. Success for whom? Right next to those sitting here, there are many others here with us, thousands of them, waiting for our success. Many of them are from our past, many from our family, who were perhaps forgotten or rejected or judged. Those waiting for some redemption, for a freedom that takes them along to another level, to another level of love, together with us. Is it all right with you if we go into this expanse?

Now it is so that every failure isn't just ours and that our complaints are not just ours either. In our symptoms others bring themselves to our attention. And they say to us: Please.

Meditation:
Confidence

Just close your eyes. We go into our body, and we become wide inside. We look at many from our family, at many from our past. We say to each one: Yes. Yes, you belong to me, and I belong to you.

We sense what changes inside us, what becomes whole in us. Suddenly our wishes move into the background, including what we had envisaged for ourselves in this course, and we feel taken along and carried by other powers.

What have we just done now? We have taken the first big step towards success, towards a big success.

Demonstration: The light

I begin with a demonstration. Who is willing to face this movement? Who dares to take this path? I look around and I know myself moved by another power. Then I choose someone. Who of you wants to work?

Hellinger chooses a man with a severe leg injury. He welcomes him and asks him to sit next to him.

HELLINGER *to this man*: Now close your eyes.
After a while: Down there, before us there are many dead people, very many. They have their eyes open. They look to you and to me. I say to them: "I know you. Many of the dead in my family lie there with you." We look at each other and we say to each other: "What are we doing here? Is there something we are supposed to do? Or do we get up, turn away, to see a light?" Suddenly we know each other alive, differently alive, at home, finally.

Now our gaze follows these dead ones into the same glowing light. We rise and take the first steps into this light. Suddenly we feel light, taken along and being carried by greater powers. We remain lost in this light.

HELLINGER *after a while to this man*: How are you?
MAN: I feel wide and solid at the same time.

HELLINGER *patting him on the shoulder*: I will do an exercise with you.

Hellinger chooses a woman as a representative and places her opposite the man, at some distance.

HELLINGER *to this woman*: Look at him.

To the man: It's from her that the help comes.

To the woman: You allow yourself to be moved as you are guided, without intention, just there.

After a while the woman squats and then sits down.

HELLINGER *to the man*: Beside her and behind her there are many more.

The woman lies down on her back.

HELLINGER *to the first row of participants in the group, around fifteen of them*: You are these others.

These representatives slowly move towards the woman who is lying on the floor. She moves away from them as far as she can. When one of the dead touches her with her foot, she screams. But the dead woman doesn't leave her alone. The other dead ones scatter. One has moved away from the others, and she looks into the distance. Most of the dead crowd around the woman on the floor. Several of them have knelt down near the woman on the floor, and are stroking her. Others look at the man on the stage. This man is very moved. One of the dead women kneels in front of him and strokes his injured leg. Then she gets up, another one stands next to her. Both look at the man. They go closer to him, and one strokes his face.

HELLINGER *after a while*: I leave it here.

Thanks to the representatives.

To the man: As you can see, you are not alone. All the best.

To the group: How are you? Did you come along with us on the path to success? Together with many, to the right and to the left of you, and behind you? And some who walk ahead?

Taken along

Close your eyes once more. We look at our life, as it was until now. How lonely perhaps, on our own. And yet we journey on in a great procession. To the left and to the right of us are many. Behind us many. We reach our hands out to the left and to the right, and suddenly we feel taken along as one of many at the same time. We imagine we take a few steps forward. With every step we leave something behind. And a few more steps, and again we leave something behind. And another step forward, and more…

Then the path goes upwards. We join in, slowly, step by step, with our gaze focused upwards, and we feel we are becoming light, lighter and lighter. We ask ourselves: Why did we carry so much? Only as weight? Now it falls away from us. We breathe deeply, take one more step forward, and up we go into a distant height.

Demonstration: The breakthrough

HELLINGER: I will do another constellation about success in life and at work. Who wants to?

To a participant: If you hadn't taken notes, I would have taken you. Writing down, we are not in touch with other powers. The heart is elsewhere, not on the paper. So, who wants to?

Hellinger chooses a woman and gets her to sit next to him.
To this woman: Close your eyes and inside, say to someone: "It is over."

After a while: And now, inside, say to this person: "I hate you."

The woman pulls a face, screams and cries loudly.

HELLINGER: This is the other side of hatred. The real feeling is different. Anyone who presents as a victim and expects pity from others (*the woman stomps her feet on the floor*) has the other feeling: wanting to kill someone. Everything else is a game.

The woman sits there with clenched teeth and a distorted face.

HELLINGER: What does such a person do as well? Commit suicide.

The woman is still stomping on the floor. After a while she calms down and breathes deeply.

HELLINGER *to the group*: Just close your eyes now. Towards whom do we behave as if we were poor sods, and a victim? Where is the death wish for the other person and for us?

The woman has calmed down and breathes deeply.

HELLINGER: How are you now?
WOMAN *after some hesitation*: I don't find the way.
HELLINGER: I have shown it to you. And I leave it at that.
After a while: How many have you already mocked inside, with these feelings?
WOMAN: Many.
HELLINGER: Exactly. This was the first step to success. All the best.

The woman smiles, relieved.

HELLINGER *to the group*: It looks as if we are on the way to success. Success is easy.

The way to success

I want to take you along into an inner movement towards success, that is, success in life. I will say something about that, so I will give a little talk. If you want to, you can close your eyes, but you can also look at me. It's the same.

The great number of success is the "two". The two wants oneness. That would be a one then. But the way to the one goes via the two. Success begins with the two. There are two, sitting side by side and holding hands. This is the way to success.

We imagine to the left of us is our mother, and to the right, our father. We stand in the middle. Our parents were two. In us, they became one. This "one" between mother and father is the greatest imaginable success. There is no greater success than a child.

The child is a one out of a two. When the child is born, he or she is a "one" in one regard, because within the child he or she joins the mother and the father into one unit. On the other hand, even though the child is a whole one, the child is born like one half of the two. The child is born as a boy or as a girl, male or female.

What happens then? After some time the boy looks for the girl, and the girl for the boy. As man and woman they want to become one. They succeed in this through a child.

Now you might think, what does he want to say with these deliberations? We are here for a course about success in life and work.

For a man, success in life begins with a woman, and for a woman it begins with a man.

Our success

Just close your eyes now. We check inside, where on our path to success in life does our father stand? Where does the man stand for the woman? Where does the woman stand for the man?

We imagine we stand in the middle between our mother to the left and our father to the right. With our mother to the left and our father to the right we move forward. We hold our mother by the hand, and we hold our father by the hand, both of them equally. Inside of us, they are always one.

The question is: Where on our path to success did our mother get lost? Where on our path to success did our father get lost? With our parents each holding one of our hands, to our left, our mother, to our right, our father, we go towards our success, with confidence.

Success is so simple, and equally obvious is the root of failure. The basic movements of life always happen between two.

The three is a sacred number. Me between my parents.

Now we will continue. How are you now, after what happened here? Are you on the path to success? Are you on the path to happiness?

I will continue as we began. I will demonstrate something in a way that all are taken along into a movement. Now I want to cross over to success in our work. Who has an issue about success in work?

Demonstration: Our profession

Hellinger chooses a client, and asks him to stand and look in the direction in front of him. Opposite the man he places a woman as the representative for his profession.

HELLINGER *to the two standing*: You just allow yourselves to be moved without any intention of your own.

The man goes towards his profession in small steps. After a while Hellinger chooses another man as a representative and asks him to lie down on his back, in front of the woman who represents success.

The client and the representative for his profession look at the dead man between them. The profession moves back a few steps. The client is now standing near the dead man on the floor.

Hellinger chooses another female representative and ask her to stand to the right of the profession. These two stand close together. The new female representative clenches her fists and looks at the dead man. Even though the two women stand close together, they do not look at each other.

HELLINGER: She is someone who is angry with the dead man. She clenches her fists.

The client walks past the feet of the dead man, and he wants to go to his profession. Suddenly he pauses, spreads his arms out, and goes backwards. The profession has slightly moved aside, and is now, from behind, leaning her head against the second woman, looking away from her. This woman looks into the distance with a tensed up face, and with her fists still clenched.

Hellinger chooses a representative for a second man, and asks him to stand where the gaze of the dead man goes.

The client has moved back from the dead man. He lifts up his shoulders and goes closer to the woman with the clenched fists. This woman backs away from the profession and stands next to the client. She is turning around in circles, as is the client, with his shoulders pulled up. After a while he turns away from this scene.

The second man stands in front of the dead man, turning his back to him. The second woman has both arms stretched out behind her, thus holding the profession tightly at her back. The profession slowly goes to the floor, and pulls the second woman with her. The profession is bending down deeply. The second woman holds one hand above her. The client stands next to them.

Hellinger chooses a third man and places him opposite the second man. A little earlier this man was standing with his legs spread apart over the dead man. The second and third men walk towards each other. The third man stretches both hands out towards the second, in an inviting gesture. The second man keeps looking back to the dead man.

After a while these two men stand together, the third man behind the second. In the meantime, the dead man has turned away.

The client is now kneeling next to the profession. The profession withdraws from him. The second woman is now lying on the floor and looks to the man. The profession has withdrawn completely.

HELLINGER: I interrupt it here. Thanks to the representatives.

Hellinger calls the client to come and sit beside him.

HELLINGER: How are you?
MAN: I feel strong. I feel this is a system that doesn't belong to me.
HELLINGER: Exactly.
To the group: What became visible here? Something from the past that does not belong to him is having an effect on this here. When something that lies far back has some influence in the present, all endeavors we make to bring some success into our enterprise are in vain.
To the man: There was a murder, quite clearly.

The man nods, and points in the direction behind him.

HELLINGER: This lies far back, the murderer wants to go; he wants to go elsewhere. Does this make sense to you?
MAN: Yes.
HELLINGER: This lies far back, and yet it is here, nevertheless. A strange sentence for the solution comes to me. Change your profession.

The man ponders on this. He turns to Hellinger, looks at him and laughs.

HELLINGER: I see it in your face: This is the future.

Both laugh at each other.

HELLINGER: All the best to you.

They shake hands.

HELLINGER *to the group*: This constellation took us along into another dimension. It was not a family constellation in the usual sense. Everything remained unsaid and mysterious. And yet, the solution was clear.

Contemplated

Close your eyes again. We look at our profession and at our enterprise through which we secure our livelihood. Where are they moving? Are they coming towards us? Are they going away from us? What do they do with their hands? Are they open? Are they closed, perhaps even clenched into a fist? What lies perhaps on the floor between us and them? Who else is perhaps joining? Who wants something from our enterprise? Something different from what we want?

We test it out internally. Where does it draw us? Into which light? Into which strength? Into which service to life? Into which joy?

After a while: Have you found a direction?

I tell you a secret about success. Do you want to know? A very deep secret: The great success is light.

There are no burdensome successes. Everything that is hard goes off the rail, like it does with love. The light love is wide – and happy.

To the group: How are you, on your way to success? When I look at your faces, many have taken this path – to easy success.

Demonstration:
Success with a partner

HELLINGER: I would like to continue, having a look at something about the success in a relationship. The great success is always the success with a partner. The great happiness as well.

Who would like to look at something in this regard, about the success with a partner?

A woman puts her hand up.

HELLINGER *to this woman*: First I ask you some questions.
   Are you married?
WOMAN: Yes.

HELLINGER: Do you have children?

WOMAN: Yes.

HELLINGER: How many?

WOMAN: Together we have four. I have two.

HELLINGER: And the other, your partner?

WOMAN: He has two.

HELLINGER: There is a former partner for your husband? Is there a former partner for you?

WOMAN: Yes. He died already.

HELLINGER: Close your eyes for a moment. Imagine you take your former partner with the left hand, and the present one with the right hand. To which partner do your children belong, to the former or to the present one?

WOMAN: To the former one.

Hellinger chooses a representative for the woman's former partner, and a woman. He places her opposite the former partner at some distance.

HELLINGER *to the client*: Are these children boys or girls?

WOMAN: A boy and a girl.

HELLINGER: Which child is older?

WOMAN: The boy.

Hellinger chooses a man for the boy and a woman for the girl.

HELLINGER *to these representatives*: Now you find your place.

The former husband takes a few steps towards the woman. Then he moves sideways. The two children stand next to him, the girl to the right, the boy to the left. Then the boy takes one step forward.

214

HELLINGER: What did your husband die from?
WOMAN: From multiple sclerosis.

The boy stands to the right of his sister. The former husband goes down to his knees. The woman looks to the left, her left hand is shaking. The woman takes a few more steps to the left. Her former husband lies down on his back. Both his arms are stretched out. The woman has both hands in front of her face, and she is crying loudly. She steps further away. In between she looks at her dead husband. She is shaking heavily and screaming loudly.

The client goes towards her representative, takes her tightly into her arms, and holds her tightly. In the meantime the son has gone down to his dead father, kneeling in front of him and holding his arm.

HELLINGER: I need one more woman.

He chooses a woman and gets her to stand somewhere apart from the rest.

HELLINGER *to this representative*: You are his death.

The client's representative has calmed down in the meantime. The client and her representative look into each other's eyes. Hellinger asks the client to sit down next to him again.

In the meantime the boy has lain down next to his father. The daughter has turned towards death and goes towards death.

The woman's representative is restless. She slowly moves towards her dead husband. The daughter keeps on looking at death. Then she turns away from him and looks to the outside.

The woman has gone past her dead husband, towards her daughter. She embraces her from behind and holds her tightly. The daughter frees herself from her mother's embrace and steps sideways. The mother reaches her hand out to her daughter.

HELLINGER: I interrupt it here.
After a while to the group: Where would your success be here?
To the client: You must go back. Otherwise your children will die.

Both look at each other for a long time. The woman gets up and returns to her seat.

HELLINGER *after a while to the group*: What can we see here? Are we free in our decisions? Is the path to our happiness open for us, as we wish it to be? Or are there other powers at work here?

Can anyone die in our place? Are we free? Or does everyone have his or her own death? Can we die for someone, so that he or she stays alive?

Overcoming

HELLINGER: Just close your eyes. We imagine several people in front of us, at some distance. Each person represents the death of another person. We look at all these people.

What happens when we just look at them? When we look at them, most deeply recollected and taken along by our life here? What happens to the representatives of other people's death? Can they stay with us? Do they become weak? Do they want to disappear?

Then what happens to us? Inside us, we turn away from them, guided by another power that rises from our heart, from another love. Leaving our weight behind, we follow another light on the wings of this love.

"Joy, great spark of God's creation,

Daughter of Elysium,
In delirious joy we enter,
Heavenly host, your sanctuary."·

After a while: How? Successfully.
Okay, this was our morning. A happy time to you!

Heaven on earth

HELLINGER: One thing above all is in the way of success. One thing above all is in the way of happiness. Something holy is in the way. This holy thing we know by the name of conscience. It is incredible that the whole occident accepted our conscience as the voice of God in our soul.

For when we look at it more closely, where does our conscience end up? It always ends up in some war. We sense inside us what happens when we follow our good conscience. Following our good conscience we always have to reject someone or even many others, even whole nations. Our good conscience always points out people to us with whom we should be angry. Can you sense that inside?

I met an Indigenous man in Canada. He told me that in his language there is no word for justice. In this tribe there is no conscience. They live without conscience. This is incredible. I asked him: "What do you do when one person has killed another?" What would we do for instance? We would scream for justice. This means, we would kill the killer.

He told me: "The victim's family adopts the one who killed the member of their tribe." They know no revenge! They move on another level of consciousness, beyond conscience.

· trans. from Schiller, Friedrich. "Ode an die Freude," 1785.

Shall I say more about conscience? It binds us to our group. Following our good conscience, we have the feeling that we are allowed to belong to our group. With our good conscience we buy the right to belong. This is the purpose and the goal of the good conscience, it binds us to our group. It binds us to our family, for instance, but also to our nation, and also to our religion. An important element is that it also forces us to reject others. So our conscience is structured in a way that we are willing to wage war against those who are seen as bad people. Every conflict, every war, is supported by the conscience that allows us, and even forces us, to see others as bad. Every bloody conflict is a war between consciences.

Our good conscience makes us feel superior to those we are supposed to reject. People with a "good conscience" must fight people who, according to their conscience, are seen as the enemy.

Tragically, the same thing happens on the other side. The other group also has a good conscience, just one that differs from ours. Therefore they reject us with their good conscience, and wage war against us with their good conscience.

And something more about conscience. Every conscience follows a god who rewards the people who follow him with heaven, and throws the other people into hell.

Then what about the god of Christendom? It is a monster of our conscience. All warring groups need to have the conscience of the group's members on their side. But if we succeed in transcending our conscience and finding our way to an all-encompassing love, then there is no more god of this kind, no god who chooses with one hand and condemns with the other.

What was the topic of our course? Ah yes, success. Success in life, success in our profession. What does success mean here? We are connected to many, with love. And – shall I say it that bluntly – connected to them with a bad conscience.

218

This is what I wanted to say as an introduction. In the constellations this morning we could already see the effect of the good conscience. This here (*he lifts up a clenched fist*) is a result of a good conscience. And this here (*he opens his arms wide*) can only be done with a bad conscience, with the farewell to our group. But this is by no means against our group, but in accord with many other groups at the same time. When we succeed in this, what do we call it then? We call it heaven on earth. Where is this heaven? Below, right down on the ground.

Demonstration:
Happiness

HELLINGER *chooses a man and asks him to sit next to him*. The way I know you so far, you look past the happiness that's near.
MAN *laughs and nods*: That's true.
HELLINGER: Now we will have a look at your happiness.
As the man becomes restless: Wait. I give myself the full time.

When I think about all the things you can do, all the things you have learned, which you have also applied successfully, and then this failure, it brings tears to my eyes.

Close your eyes. I see your happiness to your left, a woman.
To the group: I need a woman as a representative.

Hellinger chooses a woman for happiness and asks her to stand a few steps to the left of this man.

Happiness sways back and forth, bends forward and looks to the floor. With her left hand she gestures rejection. Then she straightens up, turns around backwards and moves away. Her eyes have remained closed.

HELLINGER *to the man*: Get up and let yourself be moved as you are moved from inside.

The man moves slowly towards happiness. She slowly takes a few steps further to the back. He reaches a hand out to her, and lets it sink down again. Happiness turns her head towards him. They look at each other. Then she takes a few steps backwards, but they still look at each other.

HELLINGER *choosing another representative*: You are death.

The client spreads out his arms and drops them again. He takes minute steps closer to happiness. She looks into his eyes. Death remains standing at a distance.

   Hellinger chooses a man as a representative and gets him to come on the stage, and to lie down with his back on the floor, a few meters away from the client, who looks away from him and towards happiness.

   The dead man is lying with both arms stretched out sideways. After a while the client and happiness look at this dead man.

   The client goes towards the dead man with tiny steps, bends down to him and takes his outstretched hand. The dead man embraces him and lies down again with his arms stretched out. Happiness has come up to the client and reaches out a hand to him, puts it on his head and draws him towards her. He puts his head to her tummy. She strokes him.

   Death remains standing at some distance and holds his arms stretched out. The client stretches his hand out to the dead man, but the dead man has turned his head away, to look at death. Then he turns fully away from the client.

HELLINGER: Okay, thank you all.

He asks the client to sit next to him again.

HELLINGER: Is it good like this?

The man nods, but with hesitation.

HELLINGER: Close your eyes. Imagine once more you are putting your head to the belly of happiness.

The man smiles happily.

HELLINGER: This is the movement, the only movement. Everything else you can forget. Okay now?

The man nods.

HELLINGER: All the best to you.

Family constellations of another dimension

Recently I wrote a book about family constellations of another dimension. What this is I have shown you in this workshop. It happens unknowingly, unknowingly from my side, going immediately towards an inspiration from another consciousness. Without intention, without image, guided from elsewhere. The question is: What from the earlier family constellations still counts? But you all came along, most of you came along. You have experienced personally what it means to be completely guided by another dimension, and that is always immediate, without any prior knowledge.

This dimension knows no time. It knows no preparation. When we let it lead us, we don't know time either, and the same goes for preparation. We live in the here and now. We make room for other powers, for greater powers.

What are we doing now? I don't know yet. I must let myself be guided again.

Meditation:
The next step

Just close your eyes. Now we are checking in our soul, above all, also in our heart and our soul and in our deep feeling: What would be the next step? We give ourselves the full time. The insight into the next step is light, as a very soft breeze. The feeling is immediately in our body. And it is down here on the ground.

Question: The end

How are you doing? Are there perhaps questions about this?
A woman has a question and sits next to him.

HELLINGER: What is the question?
WOMAN: During this meditation I felt completely blocked in all directions.
HELLINGER: What is the question?
WOMAN: I don't find the way. The question is: How do I find the way?
HELLINGER: I need a woman.

A woman puts her hand up and comes up to the stage. Hellinger asks the woman with the question to stand opposite this woman.

The client sways. Then she goes to the floor, lying down opposite the other woman with her arms stretched out. She bangs her hands loudly on the floor.

HELLINGER *to the group*: What do I call something like that? I call it the end.

After a while: And that's where I leave it, too.

To the representative: Thank you.

The woman with the question gets up and goes back to her seat.

Question: Conscience

HELLINGER: Now I hardly dare to ask any more who has a question. Still, does anyone else have a question?

A woman puts her hand up and sits down next to Hellinger.

WOMAN: I don't understand, or I don't know when the good or the bad conscience becomes active.

HELLINGER: Just before, with the last question, the good conscience became active. The good conscience forbids.

The inquiring woman wants to say something, but Hellinger shakes his head.

HELLINGER: And the good conscience makes you feel good.

The woman now shakes her head.

HELLINGER: And it makes others feel bad.

The woman nods.

HELLINGER: Okay, I leave it here.

To the group: It is getting more and more dangerous to ask questions!

After a while: Now I will call on greater powers again, through a constellation.

Demonstration:
The issue

HELLINGER: Who has an issue concerning success in life and success in a profession, and wants to have a look at it through constellations?

He chooses a woman and she sits down next to him. He chooses another woman as a representative and asks her to come up to the stage.

HELLINGER *to the representative*: Stand there. You are her issue.

The representative looks to the side. Hellinger chooses a male representative and asks him to stand opposite the issue at some distance, but not where she looked.

The issue turns her gaze and looks to the man. The man reaches out his right hand to her and goes towards her with the tiniest of steps. The issue begins to respond, hesitantly reaching her hand out to him. When the man has come closer to her, he reaches his hand out. After a while he puts his head on her shoulder, brings her head close to his, whilst she is still stretching out her right hand without taking the man into her arms.

HELLINGER: Okay. Thank you to the representatives.
After a while to the woman: What could we see? So much possible happiness in vain, for nothing.
To the group: The happiness we're waiting for is moving past us.

Our step

HELLINGER: Close your eyes. Now we look at a happiness for which we have been waiting for a long time, without going towards it.

After a while: Now we are waiting for someone who is standing behind us, and from whom the strength comes for our next step.

After a while: Okay.

My books

HELLINGER: I have not understood how I write my books. This has only become clear to me recently.

When I am writing a book, I am a medium. I am taken in by another movement. For instance, I wake up in the morning, and a word comes into my mind, out of the blue. Then I know, I will write a text about this word. I sit down and I write this word as the heading. Then my hand is guided, word-by-word. I do not know where it will take me. At the end comes the closing sentence that is also given to me.

Ten minutes later I have forgotten what I wrote. If I hadn't written it down, I wouldn't be able to tell any more. I even forget the heading.

This way, book after book is written. These are not my books; I am just a tool.

Why did I tell you this? These are other movements, they come from another consciousness, and they lead into another consciousness.

In this workshop we have already taken some steps into this other consciousness. And we will continue along this way.

Demonstration:
In vain

HELLINGER: Who wants to look at something concerning success in life and success in his or her profession?

A woman puts her hand up and sits next to Hellinger.

Hellinger collects himself.

HELLINGER: Two words again come to mind.
To the woman: For you. Close your eyes. I tell you these words, and you let them do their work on you. The words are: "In vain."

HELLINGER: *after a while*: I need a woman.

He chooses a woman and asks her to lie in front of the client, with her back on the floor.

He chooses a second woman and asks her to stand opposite the client so that the dead woman lies between them. After some hesitation, the second woman kneels down in front of the dead woman.

Hellinger chooses a man and asks him to stand in front of the dead woman, so that he stands a meter away from her, gazing at her head. Slowly the man goes down on his knees, takes the dead woman's head into his hands and lays his head down next to hers.

By now the second woman is lying on her back, next to the dead woman.

Hellinger asks the client to find her place amongst the representatives. She stands between the dead woman and the other woman who is lying next to her. The man clenches his fists, bangs them on the floor and cries loudly.

The client grabs his fist. She puts her other hand on the shoulder of the second woman.

This woman becomes restless and wants to free herself. As she succeeds, she turns away at first and then moves back again, but at a little distance. The man sobs loudly. He gets up and with one hand he reaches out to the hand of the client, with the other he holds the dead one.

The second woman is sitting up now. The man is still sobbing. The client takes him into her arms and holds him tight. He keeps on holding the dead woman. Then he straightens up and takes the client into his arms. The second woman sits next to the man. He also takes her up into his arms and strokes the dead woman's hair. He draws the client and the second woman's heads together and puts his in between theirs. Then he looks up to the sky.

HELLINGER: Okay. Thank you to the representatives.
To the client, when she sits next to him again:
It was in vain. For you it was in vain.

They look at each other for a long time.

Our own strength

HELLINGER *to the group:* Close your eyes. I will do a meditation with you, especially with those who apply family constellations and who have sought help through family constellations. The question is: What was in vain?
After a long pause: Now we go into our own strength, only into our own strength, and we leave others with their strength. We look beyond our life into an infinite emptiness and we remain silent.

What happens to us? Before this emptiness we are still.

What happens to our feet? We sense the earth under our feet.

What happens to our feet after a while? Where do they gain a firm stand, whilst we look into this emptiness? Only on the ground do we stand firm. There, taken along into something infinite, and we in between.

After a while: Okay. How are you?

Emptiness

I will do one more meditation with you. I will explain it first.

You imagine you stand in front of many dead from your past, those whom you have been once. Many lives stand before us.

Now close your eyes. While these dead are standing before us they are also inside us, in us and opposite us at once.

What happens to them? Do they become less? Do we become small? Do we become unimportant? Do our ideas become ridiculous?

We look beyond them into an infinite emptiness. We forget those who stood before us, who looked for a place and for help, in our body and in our mind.

While we gaze into this infinite emptiness, exposing ourselves to it, continuously exposing ourselves to it, completely exposing ourselves, neither looking to the right nor to the left, nor behind us, all those who were connected to us are also turning to this emptiness. They move beyond this emptiness, whilst we stay behind, here where we are now. We find the new freedom.

Mystic Consciousness (II)

Workshop in Milano, Italy 2013

Introduction

HELLINGER: I cordially welcome you to this course, which has the strange topic: The mystic dimensions of family constellations. I will demonstrate this. I will begin to demonstrate it so that you get an idea and are also taken along into this dimension. Is this okay with you?

In the description of this workshop there is a subtitle for the first day. It says: Mystic consciousness in action. This means: I demonstrate healing via another dimension.

Are there any of you here who would like to work with me this way? Put up your hands, then I will choose a few.

Hellinger chooses three people and asks them to sit next to him.

First demonstration:
"Now it is enough"

HELLINGER *to the first woman*: Close your eyes and, inside, say to someone: "Now it is enough."
After a while, as the woman looks across to him: Go and sit back at your place.
To the group: More I wasn't allowed to do.

When I say something like that to someone, I need no information. I get a hint from somewhere else, about what is due. At the same time I said it to all of you here. You can join in when I say something like this. You can sense whether you are open for this or not. Whether you can trust a spiritual power, or whether you move in a field where something is done by us as in the usual family constellations. In the usual family constellations, people come to me with the request that I do something for them, and that I do it the way they would like me to.

In whose service am I then? Am I in connection with a spiritual dimension? Here I move on another level.

It was helpful that she did not react. In this regard she was a lesson for all. She was acting in a helpful way for many of us. At the same time be forewarned: Here we move on another level.

Second demonstration:
"Now I stop"

HELLINGER *to the second woman*: What is the issue?
WOMAN: It's about difficulties, one after the other, in health and in work.
HELLINGER: Where is your love?

The woman nods pensively.

HELLINGER: Close your eyes. I will tell you a sentence. You repeat it inside, as it is.
To the group: You can do it too.
The sentence is: "Now I stop."

The woman breathes deeply. Then she begins to cry. She opens her eyes and closes them again.

HELLINGER *as she opens her eyes again*: Keep your eyes closed.
To the group: I will pose a question to her and to you all. She doesn't have to answer the question. Not for me.

How many people are feeling better through this sentence? How many became free?

The woman nods.

HELLINGER: Okay like that?

WOMAN: Thank you.

About the procedure

HELLINGER *to the group*: What is the procedure?

I don't need to look at the persons. When I collect myself, I am in accord with them through another power, through a healing power, through a creative power. In this spiritual dimension there are no winners who want to gain something for themselves.

Here, love flows to everyone equally. This power has immediate effect. On this level there are no games.

Just close your eyes. Imagine: What in you and in your relationships is waiting for you that you now let go – forever?

I want to say something else about this. The symptoms that many have, the problems that many have, come from possession. This means other spirits take hold of them, the spirits of earlier humans, because something remained incomplete. Now they possess us, through a symptom for instance.

Sense in yourself which symptom is in the foreground. You ask the symptom, or you ask of it: "Please tell me who you are." We wait for an answer and we ask the symptom: "What will free you?"

Instead of looking at the person or at this symptom, we wait until we are taken along into another level, the level in which the person who is speaking through our symptom finds peace and healing. Then we come into another recollection, into a collected power.

What takes place in us then? We find our way to a health, to a universal health, that connects us with many. Together we look far beyond ourselves and our world. We have a sane outlook then.

We look at this power, devoid of power, beyond our wishes, the same as all others, with all others. Devoid of self, self-less, the same as all others.

How are you feeling in this? Were you taken along to another level, to a happy level?

Third demonstration:
You are better –
now we are the same

HELLINGER *to the third woman*: Now it's your turn. What is your issue?

WOMAN: It is about the relationship with my partner that does not work any more.

HELLINGER: Okay, close your eyes. I give you a sentence that you can say to him inside. When I say it, you instantly also say this sentence to him.

To the group: You can join in, it's best to do it in an open body posture, without crossing your arms or legs, or leaving the eyes open for fear of what might happen or might get lost. Close your eyes, too.

To the woman: The sentence that came to me is: "You are better."

After a while: If you succeeded with this sentence, only if you succeeded, you tell him a second sentence. The sentence is: "Now we are equal."

After a while: All right?

WOMAN: All right.

HELLINGER *to the group*: This was preempting the topic that will occupy the day tomorrow, the main topic in life: men and women.

How are you doing with mystic consciousness in action? I didn't do a family constellation. On this level one does not need it any more. Nevertheless, where it is appropriate I will show an issue through family constellations.

The earlier and the advanced family constellations

I'll say something else about this dimension. Family constellations began with the observations of the representatives. In a family constellation, where it was directly about a family (that means parents and children), the representatives entered into direct connection with them without knowing anything about them at all.

Here I also entered into direct contact with the individuals, sometimes without having asked anything. But even then this connection became clear. How else could the representatives in a constellation know things precisely about the family and behave and feel accordingly? They came into contact with another level of consciousness; this means a consciousness that transcends our normal knowledge and capacity by far.

In the beginning of family constellations, many constellators intervened. I did it, too, because I was not fully aware of the scope of this experience.

In this regard many constellators behaved like psychotherapists, in the sense of: Tell me your problem, and I will look for a solution. This turned into a relationship between you and me, as is usual in psychotherapy. This included certain ideas about right or wrong. These ideas I have described in my first big book: *Orders of Love*. Much of what is in this book is still helpful today.

Here I don't need to refer to these orders. With what I have done here, there's no need to refer to them. In spiritual family constellations, I move beyond these orders, towards another level. Many who are used to the earlier family constellations are fearful of this level. It frightens many who are engaged in training to become family constellation practitioners, who refer to the earlier family constellations and move within the earlier family constellations.

But the earlier form of family constellations is still helpful. It is helpful to know about it and to experience it. Therefore the training that we offer in this regard still has its place, a preliminary place. Here I am going beyond this level, and I take you along if you wish.

Shall I say more about it? Many who are tied to the earlier family constellations are in the grip of a deep fear when they hear of this movement to another level. Yet in the long run they cannot avoid this movement, for the future lies elsewhere. Those of you who were or are in a training, I take you along to this other level. Others who haven't heard about it yet I am taking along anyway, right now.

Questions

HELLINGER: Are there questions about what you experienced so far?

To the woman from the first demonstration: What was the problem that occupied you? Why did you put your hand up?

WOMAN: What we have heard about the mediumistic family constellations: Does this mean that constellations take a totally new path?

HELLINGER: Yes. But my question was: What was your issue when you came here before?

WOMAN: I came here because I wanted to have a look at my relationship with my family.

HELLINGER: What for?

WOMAN: It was really about the work with my family.

HELLINGER: Just go and stand there.

She stands at some distance in the empty semicircle in the middle of the group.

235

Hellinger chooses a female representative and asks her to stand opposite the client, at some distance. The client stands immovably opposite the other woman for a long time.

HELLINGER *to the group*: What could we see? There was no movement. What was the sentence that I gave her at the beginning? The sentence was: Now it is enough. It shows up, now it is also enough here. I have shown her everything.

Are there any more questions about what took place here until now?

WOMAN: The question is not quite clear. I would like to know if these new family constellations will replace the individual constellations?

HELLINGER: I just applied it then.

WOMAN: Does this mean it all remains valid?

HELLINGER: Not everything. The essential always shows up in the beginning. Here everything showed up immediately. Everything was in the sentence that I told her. Okay?

She nods.

Story: The honor

HELLINGER: Many years ago a story came to my mind. I didn't yet grasp its dimensions then. Shall I tell you the story?

Two people sat down together, and they posed themselves the question: How would Jesus have responded if he had called out to a sick man, "Pick up your bed and walk," and the man had answered, "But I don't want to."

After a while one of them said: "Jesus would probably have remained silent at first. Then he would have said to his disciples: He honors God more than I do."

Good, on we go with the new way of short therapies. Who dares?

Hellinger chooses three people and has them sit next to him.

Fourth demonstration:
I deserved it

HELLINGER *to the first*: What is it with you?

WOMAN: It's about my income. I do not earn enough to keep myself alive with it.

HELLINGER: Close your eyes and say inside: "I deserved it.".

After a while: I leave it here. You can sit down again.

To the group: From her side, this was a game. From mine also. On this level games don't work.

Fifth demonstration:
Well done

HELLINGER *to the next*: What is your issue?

WOMAN: I have problems with my hands.

HELLINGER: What kind of problems?

WOMAN: I have a special deformation of my fingers and also arthritis in my fingers.

HELLINGER: Close your eyes.

After a while: I don't get a sentence. I respect this hint. You can sit down again.

To the translator: But I got an answer for me: Well done.

Laughing in the group.

Yes, we get feedback beyond all games.

Sixth demonstration:
Dealing with a game

HELLINGER *to the third*: What is your issue?

WOMAN: The seminar in Bozen has triggered very deep movements in me, which caused very bad pain in my back and my legs.

HELLINGER *to the group*: How did she speak to me? Was it a serious matter? It wasn't. She played with me. I noticed her laughing. Therefore I leave it here.

Going with this spiritual movement only permits full earnestness and full commitment to walk another path. It also demands of me and of you, provided you really want to get involved, full awe. Of what? Of life and death.

Any brave ones left? It was helpful to experience this here. Therefore it also makes us cautious. Then this trivial level, "Come on, do this for me," comes to an end.

Who is prepared to face this?

Three participants raise their hands. They sit down next to Hellinger.

Seventh demonstration:
"Oh that I recognized you so late!"

HELLINGER *to the first, a man*: Close your eyes. A very simple sentence comes to me. You can all join in, and go with it. The sentence is: "Oh that I recognized you so late!"

The participant cries.

HELLINGER *after a while*: Okay?
To the group: When I follow this sentence inside me, also in my life, tears come to my eyes.

Eighth demonstration:
Now that's the end of it

HELLINGER *to the next, a woman*: Collect yourself. Imagine you stomp on the floor and you scream at someone: "Now that's the end of it." But you do it without saying it. Action is enough. Okay.
To the group: The spiritual is powerful, without being angry.

Ninth demonstration:
I shit on you

HELLINGER *to the third*: What is your issue?
MAN: It goes exactly there. On the one hand I feel drawn there, to the spiritual side...

As he wants to keep on talking, Hellinger makes a dismissive gesture.

HELLINGER: Close your eyes and say to this side: "I shit on you."

How is this for you?

MAN: Different. I feel different.

HELLINGER: Different is good. All the best to you.

To the group: The spiritual, the level of the spirit, is turned to the world. It is the world. It is worldly.

Tenth demonstration:
I stop here

HELLINGER: Any questions about what went on up to now?

A woman sits down next to him.

HELLINGER: Close your eyes and say to someone: "I stop here."

After a while: Okay. Has your question been answered?

She laughs.

Eleventh demonstration:
It is enough

(Mystic consciousness applied to an illness)

HELLINGER: I would like to say something about the words "mystic consciousness." They mean: Guided from another plane. Here we leave the level of conventional family constellations. So now I would like to demonstrate the mediumistic family constellations, in connection with mediumistic short therapies. Here, it is about therapy; this means illnesses above all. Who wants to work with me in this manner?

HELLINGER *to a woman who has put her hand up*: What is your issue?

WOMAN: It is about a posttraumatic stress symptom.

HELLINGER: I don't know what that is. But I will set it up.

Hellinger chooses a representative for the woman and another female representative, whom he asks to lie down with her back on the floor, in front of the woman.

The woman wants to go to the dead woman. The dead woman spins herself around several times, away from the woman, and holds her hands in front of her face.

HELLINGER: Stop. Everything has shown up.

All go back to their places.

HELLINGER: Both representatives were in connection with another plane, without knowing what was going on. But the woman knew what it was about. That's enough.

Twelfth demonstration:
The right side

HELLINGER: Any others who want to experience this way of family constellations, and expose themselves to it?

A man puts his hand up and sits next to Hellinger.

HELLINGER *to this man*: What in your life is holding you back?

MAN: The right side, the right part.

HELLINGER: Okay, then go and stand there.

Hellinger chooses a male representative and asks him to stand opposite the client.

HELLINGER *to the representative*: You are his right part.

The representative steps aside a little, and turns his back to this man. The man becomes restless and moves back a few steps.

HELLINGER: Does the right part have a future? No. It already moved away from him. Okay, that's it already.

Hellinger asks the man to sit down next to him once more.

HELLINGER: Do you have children?
MAN: No.
HELLINGER: There was the same movement.
As he wants to turn to Hellinger: You don't need to say anything. But there is a connection. Can I leave it there?
MAN: Yes, it is enough.

HELLINGER *to the group*: It did move him. So something was set in motion in him, and this will reach the goal.
To the group: How are you doing with these mediumistic short therapies? What does this require of us? It requires one thing. Going there. That's all.

Thirteenth demonstration:
You rascal

HELLINGER: Anyone else who wants to do something with me?

A woman puts her hand up. She sits down next to him.

HELLINGER *to this woman*: Close your eyes and say to someone, just internally, but still loudly: "You rascal."

The woman looks up, closes her eyes, and is visibly moved.

HELLINGER *after a while*: Okay.

Exercise: The decisive word

HELLINGER *to the group*: I'll still do a little exercise with you.

Close your eyes and look around in the circle of those who belong to you. And you discover someone who is waiting for a word from you. The word the person is waiting for I will tell you, and you say it to this person from your inner depth. This word is: "Yes."

Man and Woman, Past and Future

Open day in Milan 2013

Story to begin:
Two kinds of happiness

HELLINGER: Buongiorno: A little bit of Italian I do know. But I speak through the eyes. And sometimes I tell stories. Stories about men and women, and perhaps you can read something in them for your own relationships.

Where do we experience the great happiness? In a couple relationship. The happiness for the man is the woman, and the happiness for the woman, such is my hope, is the man. There are of course many difficulties between them. Today I will attend to these difficulties, and we will search for a good solution together.

The story that I will tell you is called: Two kinds of happiness. One happiness is the happiness between man and woman, in a special way. The second part, too, but with certain differences. Shall I begin and tell you the story? Are you listening? Okay.

In ancient days, when the gods still seemed to be nearby, there were two bards living in the same small town, and both of them had the name of Orpheus. One of them was the big one. He had invented the kithara, an early version of the guitar, and when he touched the strings and began to sing, all living creatures in the vicinity were mesmerized. Wild animals lay calmly at his feet. Tall trees bent down to him. Nothing could resist the magic of his songs.

Because he was such a great man he wooed the most beautiful woman. That's how it goes with those great men. Then he picked up the full chalice, the woman was the full chalice, and he brought it to his mouth and wanted to drink. But while he was lifting the chalice, it broke. While he was still celebrating his wedding to the beautiful Eurydice, she died, and the great happiness was over.

245

But for the great Orpheus death was no obstacle. With the aid of his high art he found the entry to the underworld, descended into the realm of the shadows, crossed the river of forgetting, passed the hellhound, and finally he stood before the throne of the god of the dead, and melted him with his song. The god of the dead released Eurydice. But on one condition.

Orpheus was so happy that the sinister generosity of the god of the dead escaped him. He set out on the return journey, and behind him, he heard the steps of his beloved wife. They safely passed the hellhound, crossed the river of forgetting, and began the ascent to the light, which was already visible from afar.

Then Orpheus heard a scream, and startled, he turned around, to just see a shadow falling, and he was alone.

Heartbroken, he sang the song of farewell: "Oh my darling Eurydice, all my happiness is gone now."

He reached the light again, but life had become a stranger to him in the world of the dead. When drunken women wanted to take him to the feast of the new wine, he refused, and they tore him up alive.

So great was his misfortune, so futile was his art. But – the whole world knows him! This was the first story.

The other Orpheus was the little one. He was just a normal bard, who sang at little festivities, played for ordinary people, and enjoyed himself doing so. As he could not live from his art, he learned a trade, and earned his money this way. He married a normal woman, had average children, sinned a little at times, and he lived to a ripe old age, dying satisfied with his life.

But nobody knows him – apart from me.

Two love stories. I rather tend to the second one.

Now I will start with the workshop.

I am honored to cordially welcome you. We have a large group with us just for today. You know that you are a part of a seminar that began yesterday and will continue tomorrow. Today we will have a special topic that you all know well, the old theme: Man and woman, here with the addition: Past and future.

The one out of the two

HELLINGER: The first experience of man and woman we had with our parents. You can close your eyes now.

We imagine our mother standing to our left, and our father to our right. We stand in the middle and we hold hands with both parents.

In us, mother and father became one. Through our parents, each one of us is both male and female. The male and the female are inseparably united in us.

Then we were born. Even though the male and the female are inseparably joined in us as one, we are born either male, as a boy, or female, as a girl. So the original oneness has been taken apart again. But because we are originally one, both man and woman, we seek to restore the original union. Therefore the man looks for a woman, and the woman for a man. As man and woman they become one in sexual union. The result is a child. In the child they are one again.

The union of man and woman is the essential thing in life. Nothing is greater! Nothing is more fertile! Nothing is more divine!

In the bible there is a report about the creation of the human being. There is the passage: "God created man in his image." Then we are told what kind of image this is: "He created them as man and woman." For God, man and woman together are his image. This would be the foundation.

Reality

What does it look like in real life? How many men oppose women! How many men have suppressed women in the past, turning them into their subjects, brutally ruling over them! Where is the union in this? Even to this day?

So what would be important in the relationship between man and woman is the union in each way, in every regard. This union is the essential way of worshipping God. Nothing can be more religious. Nothing connects us more intensely with yonder hidden power of creation, whence all love pours forth.

This was my introduction, so to speak. We know how many obstacles there are to be overcome, before we can restore the union and live it happily.

A practical demonstration

HELLINGER: Now I would like to demonstrate through family constellations how this union can be found again, and how it can be lived. The easiest way would be to work with a couple, if a man and a woman are here together. Then they could look at their situation together and see what serves their union. Are you okay with this?

Hellinger chooses a couple who wanted to work and he asks them to sit next to him.

HELLINGER *to the group*: So, this workshop is about an advanced way of family constellations. This is a mode that restricts itself to what is essential. And I need not know anything about them. Everything essential comes to light through the work.
To the couple: Are you okay if I work like that?

COUPLE: Yes.

To the group: This way they are also protected. The personal is protected.

Hellinger chooses a representative for the man and a representative for the woman. He asks them to stand opposite each other.

To the representatives: Now you let yourself be moved as it comes from inside, without words.

The woman puts her right hand in front of her chest and breathes deeply. She grabs her head with one hand as if in distress and then puts both hands on her cheeks.

The man has his arms wide open towards her, and he staggers towards the woman. She reaches one hand out to him, then both hands, and then she drops them again. The man is still moving closer to her. They look into each other's eyes, but don't move closer. Then they take one another by the hand and continue looking intensely into each other's eyes.

Hellinger asks another woman to join the two. She stands at some distance.

The man looks over to her. His wife now moves to his left side. They both look at the second woman.

The man is standing with his arms spread. His wife has put her arm around him from behind. Then she steps back a little. The man goes to the second woman with his arms slightly open. The two smile at each other. After a while the other woman turns away and recedes.

The couple turn to each other again. After a while the man looks beyond his wife. She moves away from him slowly.

HELLINGER: Okay. Thank you
After a while to the woman: How are you?

WOMAN *laughs*: Not so good.
HELLINGER *to the man*: And how about you?
MAN: I am touched.
HELLINGER *to the couple*: Do stay here.
To the group: How do you feel when you look at that?

The past

Each love has a past. One of the important insights I had was that a lifelong connection is formed with the first sexual contact. This also holds true even when there is abuse. Wherever there was an early sexual contact between the little daughter and the father, or the little boy with the mother, a lifelong connection ensues. Of course this also applies when we are older and come into sexual contact with a partner. When there is sexual consummation, a lifelong connection remains. This shows us how elementary is the sexual act, that it forces our life into a track. We remain tied to our first sexual partner for all of our life.

In this constellation we could see that there was something that gets in the way of the present relationship.

Can you still listen? After all, this is a topic that concerns us all. The question is, where to from here? Is there a solution to this?

The solution is possible if the former relationships are acknowledged as a part of us. This applies especially to the first sexual relationship, including incest.

Now I have put my foot in. I am exposed to a lot of hostilities in this regard. When I set this up, it becomes clear that there is an original, deep love. Even if the first relationship was violent, this does not make a difference. Then the solution is the acknowledgment that there is love. It is not always an emotional love; it is a basic one in which man and woman become one. From then on the two remain tied to each other for a whole life.

Those who fight and condemn this destroy the future of the people concerned. Their later relationships have little or no future. But when it is acknowledged that this is also an act of life that not only took in our spirit, but also our body, then we can release ourselves from this first relationship, by taking it along into a later one. And the idea of the monogamous marriage is completely unrealistic concerning real life. Reality is different, and happiness too.

Our former relationships

HELLINGER: I will do a little exercise with you. Just close your eyes.

We go back into our life, back to our first relationship. However it was, we take it into our heart, exactly as it was. We feel how it still has an effect on our body and our soul.

When we have taken it into our heart and our body, we go to our next sexual relationship, however it was, and we take it into our heart. It remains in us. We have matured through them, more man and more woman.

And we go to the next one, the next one, the next one, all the way to our present connection as man and woman.

What changes if the past is allowed to come along? But without telling our partner! We do not tell except where it is official, that is, a former official relationship, such as a marriage. But even there, without telling our partner anything intimate, or asking our partner about anything intimate in their relationships.

It remains something "personal" and something "sacred."

To the couple: Okay, now you can go back.

To the group: How are you? What happened now? Shall I tell you? It was a divine service.

Family constellations of another level

Something else is worth considering here. This is a family constellation of another level. This life that we live here now is one of many. There were lives before, probably many, and also many relationships. They are still with us, to this day.

Sometimes in a relationship there is something that makes us shake our head in disbelief, something from another life is bringing itself to our attention. If we know that, we can be more careful.

Can you still listen? Shall we continue?

The double displacement

The background of many quarrels between man and woman has something to do with what happened in their family earlier on.

Sometimes, looking at couples, they suddenly have an argument that an outsider cannot grasp. It is always the same argument. It has something to do with what happened in the family. I will give you an example.

I participated in a workshop of Jirina Prekop. She demonstrated holding therapy with children, and she also wanted to demonstrate this holding between partners.

So there on the floor was a couple lying down, man and woman. Suddenly the woman's face changed, she looked like an 80-year-old woman. I asked her to hold on to this facial expression a bit longer and asked whose face she had taken on. She said it was the face of her grandmother. I asked her what happened to the grandmother.

The grandfather had a pub, together with the grandmother. Sometimes he dragged his wife through the pub by her hair, in full view of the guests! Terrible, yes?

Can you imagine this woman's feelings? No! Could she ever express her feelings? No! But these feelings are there and want to be shown. And now this woman, her granddaughter, has taken on her grandmother's feelings. This is a displacement. From the grandmother to the granddaughter. Now she must express these feelings.

And she expresses them towards her husband. He is completely innocent. But because he loves her, he puts up with it. This is also a displacement, here, from the woman to her husband.

This is the dynamic of the double displacement. Whenever you see a couple who constantly fight about the same thing—perhaps you are like that yourselves, so that this happens in your relationship—and you know this dynamic, there must be a separation. In this case, the woman must separate from her grandmother. The woman, instead of trying to avenge her grandmother, leaves this feeling with the grandmother. Or else she puts herself above the grandmother. So she leaves this old trouble with the grandmother. Then she looks at her husband, not at the grandfather, only at her husband. Then their relationship as a couple can succeed.

There's still a lot to say and to show, how we can resolve such matters, how from unhappiness happiness can rise again.

A place in your hearts

HELLINGER: We continue. This course is also about family constellations. I would like to work with a couple once more, and demonstrate this. For instance about power plays in a couple relationship. Generally about power between men and women, and how we can overcome this in a good way. Is there a couple that wants to work with me?

Two men put their hands up.

HELLINGER: Are you a couple?
FIRST MAN: Yes!
HELLINGER: For how long?
FIRST MAN: For one and a half years.

Hellinger chooses two men as representatives.
To these representatives: Stand opposite, and then we will see what is going on.

One man goes slowly towards the other. Then he goes back to where he stood before, turns to the side and looks to the floor.

HELLINGER: I need a woman.

He chooses a woman and asks her to lie in front of this man with her back on the floor.
The man goes slowly in her direction. The woman puts one hand on her chest, and the other to her throat. Then she reaches out to him with one hand and holds his foot. Then she also holds his other foot for a while. After a while she withdraws both her hands again.

HELLINGER: I need one more woman.

He chooses another woman and asks her to lie in front of the other man, with her back on the floor.
This other woman on the floor cramps up her hands and looks to the side, away from this second man.

The first woman also cramps up her hands now. She reaches over to grab the first man's foot and pushes him away. The man bends down to her and goes on his knees.

In the meantime the second man has also knelt down in front of the second woman on the floor. This woman spreads her arms out as if she was looking for something with them. Then she also puts one hand on her throat.

The first woman also puts one hand on her throat, and later she holds both hands over her head. Then the second man lies down next to the second woman. She turns away from him, and reaches over to her left as if she wanted to go to someone.

The first man is now kneeling on both knees, in front of the first woman on the floor. After a while she hits the man's legs from the side. The man withdraws, and on his knees he slithers to the second woman and the second man. The second man turns away from him, and towards the second woman on the floor. She strokes his head, but then withdraws and looks away from him, though with one hand she is still touching him. He nudges over to her and takes her hand.

In the meantime, the first woman has slowly been crawling over to the second one. Both touch one another and hold each other by the hand.

HELLINGER: I think I can leave it here. Thank you to the representatives.

To the first man: How are you?

FIRST MAN: I am broken.

HELLINGER *to the second man*: And how are you?

SECOND MAN: I have a huge amount of movement here in my belly.

HELLINGER: I haven't done anything like that before. And I don't have an image either. But without women, life is impossible,

255

without these dead women of course. They play a role. They need a place in your hearts, whatever happened in the past. Then something in your life can move, whenever. Here we have been led by another dimension. All the best to you.

THE TWO MEN: Thank you.

HELLINGER: Now you can go back.

An image

HELLINGER: I have a strange image. I will say it as it came to me. So, homosexuality is on the advance, independently of what the individual may want. The individuals are taken into service by other powers.

The image that we could see here was that these two men are drawn to dead women. These women take up a central place.

I'm not sure if I shall say all of this. A new realm has opened up for me, that's how it is. I haven't thought about this and didn't imagine anything. But this movement leads us into another realm. The image that came up for me now is, the homosexual men are attracted to women who had been abused.

When we keep this in mind, what comes up first? For me, I just say it like this; the battered women come into my mind, from long, long ago. I think I leave it here for now. Something was set in motion through this constellation, here in this group.

To these two men: I am grateful to you that you had the courage to face this. This is helpful for many, for me it is also very helpful.

Power and counterforce

HELLINGER: The topic that is important to me is power, the exertion of power in couple relationships. This is a frequent occurrence. How is power exerted? How does power oppose love? Whenever power is exerted, it calls forth a counterforce. There are always two powers, opposing each other, openly or secretly. Love shatters in the face of exertion of power. And it opposes the becoming-one of man and woman.

When a couple is grabbed by love, they are no longer themselves. They are swept off their feet. Without power. People in love do not exert power. They become "one." This intimacy comes into harm's way as soon as power is brought into play. This does not only play a role in individual couples, between man and woman, but also between "men" and "women."

Earlier on I said something about displacement, through an example. In earlier times women had to endure so much injustice and violence that today's women seek sisterhood with women from former times. They take on their pain and their hatred towards men. Then they feel strong. But not for love. For something else.

The question is: What would be the solution? The solution does not lie with the individual couple, between the woman and the man. The solution is global.

Shall I keep on talking? For the women this is especially important. The solution is that women now look at the suffering of the women from earlier times; they look at the injustice they had to suffer. They look at this with humility, with respect. The earlier women were the great ones. We in the here and now, the descendants, remain small.

Then the former women can straighten up to their full size, and today's women feel these former women behind them. They feel their power and they take up their service to life, with a man by their side, not lower than the men.

By their side! Then the exertion of power comes to an end. The woman does not exert power over the man, and the man does not exert power over the woman. In this regard, they leave each other in peace.

257

They come together, have children, and together they look at their children. How do they do that?

When it is about raising children, the woman can say to her husband: "I'll be happy if our children take after you!" And the man can say to his wife: "I'll be happy if our children take after you." Imagine how the children feel. They heave a sigh of relief. Then it will be a happy family without any exertion of power. This would be the ideal.

The different consciences

HELLINGER: What is in the way? What opposes this is the fact that husband and wife come from different families. Both are tied up with their family of origin; whatever may happen, come hell or high water, they will follow their family conscience. Husband and wife have different consciences. Then the woman wants to convert her husband to her conscience, and the husband wants to convert her to his. Most quarrels are quarrels about two different consciences – and between the gods that these consciences are supposed to serve. Shall I keep on talking? I can see that what I'm saying here is dangerous.

Every conscience serves one's own god. The wife's conscience serves the god of her family. The husband's conscience serves his family's god. What does the husband have to fear if he deviates from his family's conscience? He must fear that he will end up in hell. The same goes of course for the woman in her family. It would all be so simple if there were only men and women – without their gods.

The couple relationship succeeds with departure from the gods. The man departs from his god, and from his family's god. The woman departs from her god and from her family's god. From what do they also depart? They depart from their earlier family members.

Suddenly they become free, free for each other. That would be a beautiful couple relationship.

The spiritual path

HELLINGER: I have a few minutes left. I would like to say something about an anti-couple relationship.

Everyone who takes up a so-called spiritual path enters a path away from the woman. Who of the great gurus has a wife? Where do they lead us? To the god who created man and woman? Just think about it.

Where is God then? Where is the essential? Is it above or below? It is below!

Questions and answers

HELLINGER: Are you ready for more about men and women from the perspective of these advanced family constellations?

First of all I'll give you some time for questions about what went on here in the morning. Those with a question put your hands up.

Father's daughter

WOMAN: This morning you gave us this task, or we have done this work: We looked at our relationships one after the other. I could see what my problem is. Most of my relationships were with married men.

HELLINGER: What is the question?

WOMAN: Why don't I have a man, a man who is free, for me only?

HELLINGER: You have remained a father's daughter.

WOMAN: What do I have to do, or what shall I do then?

HELLINGER: Nothing. Who has her father for a husband doesn't need anyone else.

The relationship to a partner succeeds through the separation from father and mother. Father's daughter, who wants to represent the mother for the father, so to speak, does not need another man. And she doesn't want one either.

The same goes for men who have their mother for their partner. When the mother doesn't have a good relationship to her husband, a son will represent the father.

There are some simple sentences for the solution. Shall I tell you? Well, your father says to you: "Mommy is better."
To the group: Now she tries to charm me. But I have a better wife. Is it clear to you?

The wish

WOMAN: My question is about situations between a man and woman, in which rather extreme situations can come up. May I speak of myself? If a relationship between man and woman takes on a dangerous course, and I even have the impression that there is the danger of losing my life, that I will be killed in this situation…
HELLINGER: If you stay there, then this is your wish.

Outing oneself

WOMAN: My question is: I would like to know how important it is in a couple relationship to be seen as one really is?
HELLINGER: A simple way would be to present oneself as one really is.

Brief Constellations

Constellation: Feeling sorry

HELLINGER: Now I would like to continue with our work and set up another couple. Is there a couple who wants to work with me?

To the couple who sit next to him: Are you married?

WOMAN: No.

HELLINGER: For how long have you been together?

WOMAN: For one and a half years.

HELLINGER: I will not work with you.

WOMAN: Okay, thank you.

HELLINGER: Why not? I felt sorry for the man.

Second constellation: What matters

HELLINGER: Any other brave couples? You have seen, I won't be dragged into games.

A couple put their hands up and sit down next to him.

HELLINGER: Are you married?

MAN: No.

HELLINGER: Do you have children?

MAN: The two of us don't have a child together, but I do. I have a daughter from an earlier partner.

HELLINGER: And the woman?

WOMAN: No.

HELLINGER: For how long have you been together?

MAN: For nine months.

HELLINGER: Okay, we will set this up. I need a man for him and a woman for her.

Hellinger asks them to stand opposite each other at some distance.

261

The man recedes from the woman. He turns away, puts his hands over his face and sinks to the floor. Then he lies down with both hands over his face. The woman goes towards him and strokes his back. The man is shaking heavily, and he stomps his feet on the floor. The woman still has her hand on his back.

HELLINGER: I think I can interrupt it here. We have seen what matters, and they have also seen it. Thank you to the representatives.
To the couple: All the best to you.

Former lives

HELLINGER *to the group*: When I see something like this here, behind the woman I see other women from former lives who want to achieve something through her. Behind the man I also see this, other men, also from former generations, former lives. This will be taken further now.

The question from this morning still remains with us: How do we release ourselves from our conscience? How do we release ourselves from former lives if they endanger our present one? Shall I say more about that?

The solution

It takes a course similar to the release from our conscience. This means we move away from what ties us to that life. We dissociate from the souls who occupied us in a way that we could no longer live our own life.

Continuation of the second constellation

HELLINGER *to the man*: Now you come here once more, and you stand over there.

Hellinger chooses eight representatives and asks them to find places among the others and to be moved as they are moved.

A woman lies down on her back in front of the man and opens her arms. A representative goes down to this woman and strokes her. Others also go to her. They lie down next to her and hold her. In the end they are all lying on the floor.

Hellinger goes to the man and leads him away from this group. Together they look once more at the group, and then Hellinger leads the man back to his seat next to his partner.

To this man: How are you now?

MAN: It's better.

HELLINGER: Now look back once more and then turn around again.

Hellinger calls the partner and places her opposite the man. After a while she puts her hands around his neck and then she tenderly takes him into her arms.

HELLINGER *after a while*: Okay.

To the group: How are you doing when you look at that? So, I have taken you from a narrow consciousness into a wider consciousness, to another plane.

Meditation

HELLINGER: You can also do this now, as an inner exercise, as a meditation.

Just close your eyes. Now we look at our partner, and we place him or her at some distance from us. Then we add many other persons, men and women. We observe where our partner is drawn, how these persons move. What about them appears to be unfinished?

As we could see this in this constellation, nearly all these people still want something, even though they are dead. They are still missing something and therefore they attach themselves to the living.

Now we look at them, from a distance, without coming too close to them. Then we slowly withdraw from them. We leave them as they are and where they are. Gradually we withdraw from them, farther and farther away.

Then we turn away from them and we look at our partner. Can we find the way to our partner? Or is our partner also connected to many former persons, in a way that binds him or her?

Our partner begins the same movement, looking at the dead people, and after a while, slowly withdrawing from the dead, and only then turning around to us. Now both are free.

A gift of god

HELLINGER: To what have I committed myself now? A successful couple relationship is a gift of god. We can't just simply want it. Other powers are at work here.

Questions and answers

HELLINGER: Any questions about this? Does anyone have a question?

Several participants put their hands up and sit next to Hellinger.

I have enough

HELLINGER *to a woman*: Close your eyes, and inside, say to someone: "I have enough."

To the group: You can join in here. You can also say this to someone.

After a while: Can I leave it there?

WOMAN: Yes, thank you. But I would love to say something.

HELLINGER No.

To the group: For those unfamiliar with this, it was a short therapy on another level.

It is over

WOMAN: How does this movement succeed? How can one overcome what poses an obstacle on the way to one's partner?

HELLINGER Go and stand there. Stand there and look ahead in this direction.

Hellinger chooses another woman and asks her to stand opposite the woman with the question.

The client retreats from the second woman, turns away, and puts her hand in front of her face.

Hellinger tells the second woman that she can sit down again. Then he chooses a man and asks him to stand opposite the client.

The woman walks slowly towards the man, her hand crossed over her sexual parts. She tries to touch him. He does not look at her and after a while he goes on his knees. The client keeps on trying to touch him but doesn't succeed.

Hellinger chooses a third woman and asks her to lie down in front of the man with her back on the floor, and several meters away from him. The man turns his head to the right, away from her and the client. The client crosses her hands in front of her chest and walks away from him.

She slowly goes over to the dead woman who has one hand held out to her. She tries to draw the dead woman towards her. In the meantime the man has gotten up, but now he kneels down again.

HELLINGER: What can we see here about a couple relationship, and about the chance of a couple relationship for her? It is over! The chance is over. Okay, thank you to the representatives.
To the woman: I leave it there. We have seen everything. You have seen everything.
To the group: I have summed up the chances for a couple relationship. For a woman I have summed it up. Without mother no husband.
To the first representative: You were the mother. You were the mother, and there was also a dead female. But I won't go there.
To the group: How are you doing with this? Can you still follow when it gets serious?

I stop

HELLINGER *to a woman*: Now you can ask questions.
WOMAN: What you call the uniqueness of a couple relationship, I have seen in the beginning. I still feel that inside me, but I don't see it any more, the uniqueness of a couple relationship.
HELLINGER: I don't understand this.

To the group: Did you understand the question? No? If we don't understand it, then something else has the attention.

To the woman: Close your eyes and say to someone: "I stop."

Okay?

WOMAN: Thank you.

HELLINGER: Stopping is the first step to new worlds.

The children

HELLINGER: This workshop is above all about man and woman. But what are a man and a woman without children? The children are the fulfillment of a couple relationship. The couple relationship is designed for children. Without children the couple relationship is incomplete. Nowadays many think just about man and woman when they talk about a couples relationship. In the old days it was clear, the first child arrives one year after the wedding. The purpose of the couple relationship was the child. Only through the child did it become complete. The child is the visible result of a couple relationship.

The question is, what happens to the couple relationship once they have a child? To begin with, both partners are very busy. The couple relationship grows through this.

Now the question is: Is the child allowed to belong to both? Does one of the partners draw the child closer and therefore further away from the other parent? Or is the child allowed to go back and forth between both parents? These days we can see that many women draw the child towards them. The father has done his duty so to speak, and now he can go. I exaggerate of course. The child who remains with the mother, who is pulled in by the mother, loses connection with the world. Poor child! Can you sense this? It is the father who introduces the child to the world. The father takes the child beyond the boundaries of the family, into the big wide world.

Therefore it is important that the father takes the child out into the world quite early.

Then there's something else that happens to children. Something is transferred to children. And there is the sentence, a very basic sentence that we can observe in family constellations. The mother says to the child: "You for me." It is mostly the mother who says this; it's rarely the father. What does "You for me" mean? Ultimately it means: "Die for me."

This is connected to a sense of guilt. Those who feel guilty want to punish themselves. They hope to be freed from guilt through self-inflicted punishment. Many illnesses and accidents are the result of guilt feelings. With their feelings of guilt people want to be freed from their guilt through a punishment, above all through one's own death.

When we look at Christianity we see that the whole of Christianity is based on the notion that someone must die so that some guilt will be atoned. First of all, this was ascribed to Jesus, that he had to die on the cross so that we could all be delivered from our sins.

Is this not crazy? Is this idea not crazy? And yet, in many families there is this idea that someone in the family expects another family member to die for them. Then children get sick and they feel superior in this. They say: "I will do it. I will atone for you. I am the big one here." For when the mother or someone else in the family says: "You for me," a child answers: "I for you."

Worries and concerns

HELLINGER: I had the opportunity to observe some strange things.

So, there comes a woman who says: "My son, he's 24 years old now, I am worried about him."

Now check this out in yourselves. Which of your children are you concerned about? Close your eyes.

So there is the child about whom you are worried. Now imagine, that this child dies. How are you feeling then? Better or worse?

Each worry is a death wish. What about the couple relationship then? It is over, of course. Very often a partner, mostly it is the man who says it to the woman: "I for you." And the woman says to him, secretly of course: "You for me." When the man dies, how does the woman feel? She feels better.

Demonstration:
All dead

HELLINGER: Couple relationships can be dangerous, especially for men. I think I will have to stop here. But I will just demonstrate this. Is there someone here who knows about a woman who worries about her son or daughter? I will not work with a personal issue; this would be too risky here. But we can work with someone whom we don't know and who is not present.

A woman puts her hand up and sits next to Hellinger.

HELLINGER: Is it about a man or a woman who is concerned?
WOMAN: About a woman.
HELLINGER: Is the child a boy or a girl?
WOMAN: It is a boy.

Hellinger chooses a representative for this woman and this boy. He places them opposite each other at some distance.

The woman reaches out to the son, first with one hand, and then, quite invitingly, with both.

HELLINGER: This is called a temptation.

The son sinks to his knees and lies down. The woman does the same.

HELLINGER: Here we can see the other movement. This is the result of worrying: All dead.
To the woman and the representatives: Thank you, we have seen it.

Child sacrifices

HELLINGER: Where have I ended up? Now there's a risk of attributing guilt to this woman.

Recently I wrote a book. It's been published in German, and in April or May it will come out in Italian as well. The book is called: *The Churches and Their God.*

There's a chapter about child sacrifices in this book. I followed up on that, the sacrificing of children. I am describing the history of child sacrifice. I remember, in Israel there is a historical excavation site of a temple, from a time long before the Israelites came to Canaan. There's a large stone altar for the child sacrifices. The children were slaughtered there, above all the first-born. The idea was that the parents would have a good life if they sacrificed children to a god who demanded this of them.

When the Israelites invaded Canaan, they also took on this custom. Not far from Jerusalem there was a special temple for child sacrifices. The children were sacrificed to a god called Moloch. So the parents went there. The image of this god was an oven. The oven was heated, and then the children were thrown into this oven. The parents sang as loud as they could, so that they did not hear the screaming of the children. And they hoped that now the blessings of this god would descend upon them.

Are we far removed from this imagination? Or right in the middle? How many children are sacrificed nowadays? For instance, through abortions. They are sacrificed so that the mother will be well. This is a widespread practice.

In Judaism the prophets railed against this practice, but they were not successful. It only stopped when Jerusalem was conquered by the Babylonians and the Jewish people were taken into captivity.

The question is: What about Jesus? He goes to Mount Olive, sweats blood, and prays to God: "Let this chalice pass me. But not my will be done, but yours." This will was done. Jesus died on the cross.

The Christendom that was usurped by the Romans spread this version: Jesus died to reconcile this god. Who nailed him to the cross? His henchmen? Or god, his so- called father?

These days we carry the cross of Jesus with him, we walk the Stations of the Cross, sacrifice our life to reconcile this god. Then some mothers and fathers, but above all the mothers, hope that a child will die, so that god's blessing will be evoked and fall upon them.

But then there are some ways out. They hope that a child will be dedicated to god, for instance a boy will be ordained as a priest, or a daughter enters a convent as a bride of Jesus.

Is this not crazy? The hope is that this way, god's blessing will come down on this family.

The same movement exists when one of the parents says to the children: "You for me."

I will tell you a story about this. Originally, many years ago now, I wrote about child sacrifice. At first I attributed this child sacrifice to god. But it is not god for whom this child is sacrificed. It is not god who wants this! The mother wants it, the father wants it! The question is, how do we find a way out of these dreadful

271

imaginations and actions that follow them, and into another love? Now close your eyes, and I will tell you this story.

On the one hand it is a story from the Bible, but I will go deeper into it. So this is the story:

A man dreamt at night that he heard the voice of god who said to him: "Get up, take your son, take your only, beloved son, lead him to the mountain that I will show you, and there sacrifice him to me by slaughtering him." The son's name was Isaac.

He led him to the mountain, built an altar, tied the child's hands, drew his knife, ready to kill him.

Then he heard another voice, and instead of his son, he slaughtered a sheep.

What is different in this family now?
How does the child look at his father?
How does the father look at his son?
How does the woman look at her husband?
How does the man look at his wife?
How do they look at god?
And how does god look at them – if he exists?

But who was this god? Who is this god? Only the father! Only us, if we are waiting for the death of a child so that we may be well.

Now I will continue with the story, with the resolution of the story.

Another man dreamt at night he had heard the voice of god who said to him: "Get up, take your son, take your only, beloved son, lead him to the mountain that I will show you, and there sacrifice him to me by slaughtering him."

In the morning the man got up, looked at his son, his only, beloved son, looked at his wife, his child's mother, looked at his god.

He faced him squarely and he said: "I won't do that."

How does the son look at his father now?

How does the father look at his son?

How does the woman look at her husband?

How does the man look at his wife?

How do they look at god?

And how does god – if he exists – look at them?

There is no end to child sacrifice these days, and neither to parents who are prepared to sacrifice their children.

Is anyone of us personally guilty? Or do we all move in a field of manifold ways of child sacrifice, with the sentence "You for me"?

And how do the children willingly agree to this, with the sentence: "Me for you"? And thus we move within a huge battlefield.

What is the solution now? These children who were sacrificed, in a bloody or non-bloody way, we take them all into our heart. For they are not dead, they are all there. We say to them: "Please come back!"

I have gone out on a limb. How? With love.

The future

How are you doing? The children, that was the other dimension of the couple relationship. With a view to this dimension we can take a decisive step into another future.

This workshop that will continue tomorrow takes us to another plane of consciousness, beyond good and bad.

273

Good and bad, right and wrong are inescapable to us for as long as we remain in the thrall of conscience. On this other plane our conscience ceases to be. Then there is no exertion of power over one another, neither over a partner nor over children. On this other plane everything may stay together, the way it belongs together.

This requires of us an adjustment in every regard. We can't force it. We are taken there when we cease distinguishing between good and bad. Firstly in ourselves and in our partner and in our children. On this other plane all are together and at one in a way that surpasses our concepts and our imagination by far.

Now I would like to tell you a story at the end of this course today, a true story. After this story we leave the room without talking to each other, without applause or any other sound. We return into our everyday life in recollection. How? Changed!

During a workshop in Holland to which I was invited as a guest - it was a course about organizations – the course leader suggested at the end of the course that we could set up the church as an organization. So it was his initiative, and I agreed.

I asked him to choose a female representative for the church, and he chose one. The church's representative just stood there. I let myself be guided and I said to him: Now choose a representative for Jesus. He chose a man who then came onto the stage. There was the church that looked in one direction, and this man who represented Jesus, stood there without looking at the church. He looked in a direction that bypassed the church.

Then I asked the workshop leader to choose one more man as a representative for God. The leader chose one, and the man came up some steps to the stage, but not to the top.

Jesus took some steps towards God and then some steps backwards. Then God stepped onto the stage. Neither God nor Jesus looked at the church. When God stood on the stage Jesus went towards him in small steps, and they embraced tenderly. Then

Jesus released himself from the embrace with God, and he moved away backwards, still facing God. In the meantime something happened to the church. She leaned forward very far and looked to the floor. We know from family constellations what this means. The church looked at dead people.

I chose a woman to represent these dead people, and I asked her to lie in front of the church, with her back on the floor.

Now something strange happened. God sat down on the floor next to the dead persons, and he began to cry. Then he lay down next to the dead person and closed his eyes. He, too, was dead. This was my story.

Closing Words

Movements of the spirit

HELLINGER: I would like to say something about the spirit. We don't know what that is. Some have the image that the spirit is something tangible, that it comes into direct contact with us in a special way. When I imagine this, when I try to think this through, it is obvious that the creative spirit is equally in connection with everything. Then I bid farewell to the idea that the spirit could favor me particularly. The spirit is kindly disposed towards me and to all others, to all of us together, to each one in a special way.

When we experience ourselves being taken by a spiritual movement, as you can experience it as a representative in constellations, we experience that we are taken in by another movement. Yet not in a personal way, but in the service of a movement for many at the same time. In accord with these movements we come into accord with another love, beyond our little self. Therefore we cannot interpret it as something personal, and even less so, as *especially* for us as individuals. Instead, we experience ourselves in the river of this infinite love.

Here we experience ourselves taken along into a completely different space, into a spiritual space, and into a universal consciousness. From there we receive insights that transcend our thinking by far. You have also experienced this in the exercises we did here. In this space, when we are taken in by the movements of the spirit, we leave everything behind that stands in the way of love, guilt above all.

Good and bad

Guilt has no place in this realm. And we let go of all temptations to atone for some guilt.

We experience two contrary movements inside. We don't just experience ourselves as good. The movements of the spirit foster the

277

good in the sense of serving life. At the same time these movements are also destructive. They destroy something in order to make room for something new. In this sense even wars are movements of the spirit.

I was touched when I heard from someone that the Aztecs gave everything away after 52 years, in order to make room for new things. In the Jewish religion there is also a movement of "letting go for new things."

The cruel

We experience something cruel inside, in our soul, and also in accord with a movement of the spirit. Then we want to overcome it. We want it gone. But we are all taken along into movements that do harm, that appear to do harm. For in the large-scale they serve progress and the continuation of life.

When we experience this in ourselves, when we feel this aggressive tendency, we agree to it as a movement of the spirit. Then the opposition of good and bad in our soul is uplifted and merged in a greater movement. Only in this way can we truly become one with the movements of the spirit. This is a mystical experience of oneness. This is the full mysticism where everything has its place and, ultimately, everything serves love in the end. So in this way we arrive at a completely different religious perception and attitude. When we achieve this, happiness is within reach. We can agree to everything as it is.

Good and bad spirits

There's something else that makes me wonder. For instance a song that invokes good spirits. There appears to be a realm beyond the human one, which hosts a multitude of spiritual beings, who come to our aid in the service of the higher power.

Well, we also imagine that there are guardian angels. This is not just an idea. Many of us have experienced the sudden presence of a guardian angel who helped us out of a dangerous situation. So, instead of seeking the direct connection to this spiritual power, we can also ask these good spirits to be with us.

The question is: Are there also bad spirits? This is a widespread idea that there are also bad powers at work. In family constellations we can see that the representatives of dead people can be inclined to draw the living into death with them.

Some spirits have quite bad effects on the living. For instance when they drive living persons into death and also into insanity.

Peace to the dead

What can we see in family constellations? When we give room to the movements of the spirit something changes for these dead people. In the end they let go of the living and close their eyes to complete their death. Then they leave the living in peace. And there's more. When they have found peace, they become guardian angels for the living. So, something has to be put into order for these dead ones, and they expect this help from us. Putting things into order always means: We take them into our hearts as they are, including the so-called criminals. They need to be equally taken into the family and even into the larger soul.

Now you realize that it is a movement of the spirit that all human beings are taken into this great movement, all of them as they are, whatever their guilt, whatever their fate. Of course we can only succeed in this where we can bring the good and the bad together in our soul into a mystical union, as a movement of the spirit.

Now, whether the good spirits and the bad spirits used to be humans, or whether there are still other spirits, I don't know. I tend to relate to the dead. Then I am most intimately connected with this

279

other world, and together with its dwellers, also with this eternal power.

Images of God

This eternal spirit, this divine power – I call it divine here – is not something that we can grasp with our concepts of God.

I will make a daring statement here. All of our images of God, of our dear god, of the judge, are insulting to God. They are arrogant to the nth degree. For this God is good and bad, above all, he is terrible. For the so-called dear god of love is a terrible god, of whom we must all live in fear.

This eternal God, this spiritual movement, allows no images. It allows no religion either. It allows no ritual. What is this about? What do we want to achieve with these rituals? Do we want to influence God? There are no houses of God and no intermediaries either. But there is the experience of a movement of love for all.

Do we have to be afraid? May we ask this power to help someone? Can we love more than this power? Every praying comes to an end here as well, and the same goes for wishing and fearing.

Now how do we relate to this power? Is it external? Or is it inside us? Can anything move inside us that is not coming from this power?

Then what is worshiping God? We go with this movement of life inside us. What is the summit of the religious attitude? We are just there before this eternal spirit, without any movement of our own; we are there just as we are. This is the full accomplishment for all of us.

APPENDIX

How did I come to write this book?

First, even though I became known through family constellations, I had been a teacher in South Africa for many years, teaching indigenous African school children. In my last position I was the principal of the renowned St. Francis College in Marianhill, one of the leading high schools for indigenous Africans in South Africa. I prepared myself for this position in a three-year study course at the University of Natal and the University of South Africa, finishing with the University Education Diploma. This qualified me to teach at high schools in South Africa.

Second, in South Africa I participated in the new movement concerning Group Dynamics. The participants learned, through immediate experience, according to which laws a group organizes itself in a way that considers and includes all participants. I completed the training in group dynamics, and I applied these laws successfully. They helped me to create a climate of mutual trust in which there were no outsiders.

Third, it was through family constellations that I came to the insights about the basic orders in our relationships. I have brought them together under the term Hellinger® sciencia, for they have been proven to be essential for all human relationships.

Family constellations revealed that parents and also children are embedded in greater connections in complex ways. The events in earlier generations and the whole life situation these generations were exposed to still have effects on those living now. In the Hellinger pedagogy they are brought to life in a way that all involved can breathe a sigh of relief. Another future is awaiting them, close to life and full of confidence.

In the meantime I have presented these insights in many courses for parents and children, for teachers and students, some of them together with my wife Sophie.

This book is a practical book, both for educators in institutions and schools, and for parents who seek help when their children run away. It is also a help for other helpers who are willing to support these primary caregivers and educators in many ways.

The Hellinger® sciencia

The *Hellinger® sciencia* is a science of the love of the spirit. It is a sciencia universalis, the universal language of the orders of human beings sharing their lives, beginning with the family, that is between man and woman and parents and children, including their education, and further on, to the orders in work situations, professions and organizations, and all the way to larger groups such as ethnic groups, nations, and cultures.

At the same time it is the universal science concerning the disorders that lead to conflict in human interactions of all kinds, thereby separating human beings and groups instead of bringing them together.

These orders and disorders transfer themselves also to our body. They play an important role in illnesses and in physical, emotional, and mental well-being.

As a scientific discipline the *Hellinger® sciencia* remains in motion. This means, it constantly develops further, and it does so also through the experiences and insights of many others who dedicated themselves to it, and also to its consequences. As a living science it does not form a school in the sense of being complete, as if it could be taught and learned as a canon of fixed knowledge. Its justification lies solely in its effect and success. It is and remains an open science in every way.

The spiritual dimension

The *Hellinger® sciencia* has produced insights into the orders and disorders in our relationships. They can be experienced by anyone. Beyond this, it has reached another dimension, a spiritual dimension. Only from this dimension can we appreciate the scope of these insights. Only from this dimension can we experience its universal importance, and the consequences that result from this in all spheres of life.

What is this spiritual insight, and what are its dimensions? This insight begins with an observation and what follows from it: Everything that is does not move of its own impulse. It is moved from outside. Even if it moves as if it moves by itself, like for instance everything that lives, its movement has its origin in something that cannot come from itself.

Therefore, every movement, including the movement of everything alive, goes back to a movement from outside, and that is not just at its beginning, but continuously, for the whole course of life.

There's something else to keep in mind. Every movement, especially every living movement, is a conscious movement, a known movement. It presupposes consciousness in the power that moves everything. In other words: Every movement is a movement that is thought first. It comes into motion because it was thought by this power, and it comes into motion the way it was thought.

So what is at the beginning of every power? A thinking that thinks everything as it is.

What follows from this? There is nothing for this thinking that it did not want the way it is and how it moves. Every movement is ultimately a movement of the spirit. Therefore nothing ever ends for this spirit. Everything that was, this spirit is still thinking it in the same way as it thinks us in the present, and also everything that is still to come.

As the spirit thinks the future together with the past, the past is related towards what is coming in everything. The past is moving towards what is coming, and it achieves its completion in what is coming.

But what is coming will also become something of the past, and then it also moves as something past, which means towards something that is still in the future. It is unimaginable for us, that this all-moving thinking can ever end. Just like there cannot be anything that was not thought by it, the same way there cannot ever be anything after it. For who or what should be there to think it after it?

In the face of this thinking many of our important assumptions and ideas appear futile. The assumption of a free will for instance, the assumption of personal responsibility. And many value judgments and distinctions that we see as the carriers of our culture fall away.

In the first instance I will name the distinction between good and bad, right and wrong, between chosen and rejected, between up and down, high and low, better and worse, and ultimately between life and death.

Yet we keep on making these distinctions, and we also experience them. Are they then not also thought and wanted by this spirit as they are?

There is something to consider here: The past and the coming are not the same. The past is on the way to the coming. Therefore in our experience there is a before and an after, and a more or less.

What is this less? What is this more? It is less consciousness or more consciousness. We find ourselves in a movement from less conscious towards more conscious, in accord with this spirit and its all-embracing movement, towards *"more consciously in accord with the spirit's movement."* So for us there is a movement of more or less, which is not conceivable for this spirit. And yet, this movement is there in everything we meet in it, thought by this spirit in this movement. It is thought for us this way by the spirit, whatever it may demand from us in terms of experience on the path towards more consciousness.

Who achieves this more of consciousness? Who achieves this more of accord with the consciousness of this spirit? Can this be us personally? Can we be this, just us in this life? Or are all human beings together – from past, present, and future times – on this path to achieve this consciousness together? Do they only achieve this together with all the experiences they ever had and also those that still need to be had, by us and also by so many others, in this life as well as in many others? And again, only together?

Freedom

Of course, we feel free in many regards. Of course, we feel responsible for our actions and their consequences. Yet at the same time we know that another power, a spiritual power that moves everything, has thought and moved and willed our freedom and our responsibility and our guilt with all its consequences in such a way that we experience them as our own.

Do we act differently then? Can we act differently? Where shall we find the strength to move and act differently?

So what is left for us to do? To act the same way as before, and to agree to our freedom and to our responsibility and to our past and our guilt with all its consequences, exactly as they are and as we experience them.

At the same time we also experience them as an increase in conscious accord with this all-moving spirit. We experience this accord also as a more in consciousness, for us and also for all who carry the consequences of our freedom and our responsibility with us, and who were drawn into the consequences of our actions and our guilt.

Worries

In this spiritual dimension the worries end, including the worries about the future of the *Hellinger® sciencia*. It came from a movement of the spirit and it remains in motion, the way this spirit thinks it, regardless of whether meeting with approval or rejection. As a universal science it proves its truth, either in this way or that, only through its effect.

So what about the worries we have about the future: about our future, about the future of other people, about the future of the world? Don't these worries prove themselves to be foolish, given that we can't achieve anything through them? They would be worries against the movements of the spirit as if they were independent of the spirit.

It's a different matter with the concerns that we feel in accord with the movements of this spirit. They are concerns out of care in the service of the world, as this spirit moves it. They are in accord with the spirit's concern and care. These concerns are in accord with the orders of life, with its beginning and with its end.

The future

In accord with the thinking of this spirit, every future is now for us. This spirit thinks everything now. In the spiritual dimension the concern about what is next comes to an end. Everything that is next is shown to us in accord with this movement now. Because there is a next one, there is also a future for us, but a future now.

The *Hellinger® sciencia* is a science for the now. All its insights work right now and right here. Resistances to these insights are also doing their work now and immediately. The *Hellinger® sciencia* is a science of our relationships now.

Love

Ultimately, the *Hellinger® sciencia* is a science of love. It is the science of that love that includes everything, and even in the same way.

How is this love achieved? It succeeds in accord with the thinking of the spirit that moves everything the way it thinks. It is the love in accord with the thinking of this spirit. It is aware of the movements of this spirit. This love knows how it loves and how it is allowed to love, because it becomes aware of this love through an insight in accord with the consciousness of the spirit.

Therefore this love is also pure, like this consciousness. It is pure because it is moved by another thinking. It is a knowing love, it is pure knowing love.

Therefore it is also a creative love, creative in accord with the thinking of this spirit. Therefore this love also becomes a science, a universal science. As a universal science it works universally. It works because it is true.

Hellinger Pedagogy

The Hellinger pedagogy is applied *Hellinger® sciencia*. It is *Hellinger® sciencia* applied to education in all its aspects.

Contacts

Homepage

www.Hellinger.com

Email:

info@hellingerschule.com

Online Shop

www.Hellinger-Shop.com

Learning with Hellinger

At www.Hellinger.com you will find the seminars held by Bert and Sophie Hellinger and the Hellinger School worldwide.

Made in United States
North Haven, CT
17 November 2024